Project Studio Blueprint

Project Studio Blueprint

Greg Galluccio

A Division of Prentice Hall Computer Publishing

11711 North College, Carmel, Indiana 46032 USA

International Standard Book Number: 0-672-30275-6
Library of Congress Catalog Card Number: 91-68307

94 93 92   9 8 7 6 5 4 3 2 1

Interpretation of the printing code: the rightmost number of the first series of numbers is the year of the book's printing; the rightmost number of the second series of numbers is the number of the book's printing. For example, a printing code of 92-1 shows that the first printing of the book occurred in 1992.

Screen reproductions in this book were created by means of the program Collage Plus from Inner Media, Inc., Hollis, NH.

Printed in the United States of America

Trademark Acknowledgments

Publisher
Richard K. Swadley

Associate Publisher
Marie Butler-Knight

Managing Editor
Elizabeth Keaffaber

Development Editor
Wayne Blankenbeckler

Copy Editors
Howard Peirce, Barry Childs-Helton

Editorial Assistant
Hilary Adams

Designer
Michele Laseau

Indexer
Jeanne Clark

Production Team
Paula Carroll, Brad Chinn, Keith Davenport, Mark Enochs, Joelynn Gifford, Debbie Hanna, Carrie Keesling, Betty Kish, David McKenna, Matthew Morrill, Linda Seifert, Dennis Sheehan, Suzanne Tully, Jeff Valler, Corinne Walls, Mary Beth Wakefield, Jenny Watson, Phil Worthington

***Special thanks to Kirk Butler and John Lyzott
for assuring the technical accuracy of this book.***

CONTENTS

Foreword   *xiii*

Introduction   *xv*

Acknowledgments   *xvii*

1   **The Design Process: Getting It Down On Paper** *1*
The Business of Recording, 2
A Caution About Zoning, 3
The Range of Possibilities, 4
Use of Space, 5
Planning Your Space, 7
    Access, 7
    Soundproofing, 8
    Wire Routing, 9
    Maintenance Access, 9
    Acoustics, 10
    Equipment Layout and Ergonomics, 11
    Heating, Ventilation and Air Conditioning, 11
    Isolation Booth, 12
    Plumbing, 12
Workspace Examples, 12
A Final Note, 19

2   **Studio Equipment: Making the Right Decisions**   *21*
Compatibility, 22
The State of the Art, 23
The Modern Recording Process, 24

Analog Multitrack Tape Recorders, 26
MIDI Sequencing Equipment, 31
Samplers, 35
Synchronizers, 38
The Mixing Console, 39
Outboard Effects, 44
Mixdown Decks, 46
Digital Audio Workstations, 47
The Monitoring Section, 49
Microphones, 53
Test and Maintenance Equipment, 55
Summary, 56

3   **Budgeting: All Those Things You Didn't Think About** *59*

Budget Considerations, 60
   Audio Wire and Cable, 60
   Racks and Stands, 62
   Furnishings, 63
   Outside Services, 63
   Equipment Service Contracts, 64
   Sales Tax, 64
Putting Together a Rough Estimate Budget, 64
Calculating Construction Costs, 68
Related Expenses, 69
Insurance, 70
Dealing with Dealers, 71
Financing, 72
   Unsecured Personal Loans, 72
   Business Loans, 73
   Home Equity Loans, 73
   Venture Capital, 73
Summary, 74

4   **Construction: Acoustic Considerations and Techniques** *75*

The Nature of Sound, 76
Construction Materials, 76
   Weather Stripping, 77

Carpeting, 77
Acoustic Foam, 77
Wallboard, 78
Lumber, 78
Concrete, 78
Fiberglass Insulation, 79
Wall Construction Techniques, 79
Soundproof Walls, 80
Soundproof Ceilings, 82
Soundproof Windows, 84
The Sound Lock, 88
The Isolation Booth, 89
Wire Routing, 90
Equipment Racks, 91
Climate Control, 92
Other Considerations, 93
Summary, 93

5   Electrical Circuits: Power and Audio   *95*
Power Circuits, 95
Determining Requirements, 97
Separation of Circuits, 99
Grounding Power Circuits, 100
Lighting, 102
Other Considerations, 103
Audio Circuits, 104
Wiring Requirements, 104
Balanced versus Unbalanced Wiring, 106
Types of Wire, 108
Labelling, 109
Studio Input Stations, 109
How to Construct a Headphone Distribution
System, 111
Other Circuits, 112
Summary, 113

6   The Audio Patch Bay   *115*
Patch Bay Types, 116
Laying Out the Patch Bay, 120

Soldering, 125
    Soldering Tools, 125
    Soldering Techniques, 126
Patch Cords and Plugs, 129
Summary, 129

7   **Acoustics** *131*
The Monitoring Area, 132
    Reverberation Time, 133
    Diffusion, 135
    Live End Dead End Design, 136
    Equalization?, 141
    Measurements, 142
The Recording Area, 142
Your Ears Are the Judge, 143
Summary, 144

8   **Construction: Finishing Touches** *147*
Preparation, 147
Equipment Racks and Stands, 148
    Special Grounding Considerations, 148
    Rack Constructions, 150
Empty Spaces, 154
Equipment Cabinets, 156
Monitor Mounting, 158
Microphone Mounting, 160
Security Systems, 161
    Sensors, 161
    Control Panels, 162
    Audible and Inaudible Alarms, 162
Acoustic Foam, 163
Chairs and Other Furniture, 163
Summary, 164

9   **The Fun Stuff: Installation and Troubleshooting** *165*
Unpacking, 166
Testing the Equipment, 167
    Checkout Procedures, 168

Paperwork, 171
Installation, 173
   Eliminating Grounding Problems, 173
   High-Frequency Noise, 174
System Check, 175
   Console and Multitrack, 175
   Studio Functions, 176
   Patch Bay and Peripheral Equipment, 176
Maintenance and Repair, 178
   Cleaning the Tape Path, 178
   Demagnetizing, 179
   Tape Deck Calibration and Nonroutine Adjustments, 180
   Repair Work, 181
Smoking, 182
Summary, 182

10   Going Multimedia   *183*

Audio for Video, 184
Synchronization, 186
   SMPTE Time Code, 186
Other Audio, 188
Video Standards, 188
What's Next?, 190

11   The Studio Business   *191*

Zoning Laws, 192
The Business Plan, 193
The Small Business Development Center, 193
To Incorporate or Not To Incorporate, 194
   Sole Proprietorship, 194
   Partnerships, 194
   Corporations, 195
Taxes, 196
Advertising, 196
   Press Releases, 197
   Magazines and Publications, 198
   Advertising Agencies, 198
   Direct-Mail Marketing, 198
   Public Relations, 199

Pricing, 199
    Terms and Conditions, 200
Epilogue, 204

Appendixes

A   Resources   *207*
Bibliography, 208

B   Sample Business Plan   *211*
The Three-Year Business Plan, 212
    Summary, 212
    Purpose, 213
Table of Contents, 214
I. The Business, 214
    A. Business Description, 214
    B. Products or Services, 215
    C. Management Plan, 215
    D. Operations Plan, 216
    E. Risks, 218
II. Marketing Plan, 218
    A. Marketing Research, 218
    B. Objectives and Strategy, 219
    C. Pricing Policy, 220
    D. Sales Terms, 220
    E. Method of Sales and Distribution, 220
    F. Customer Service, 220
    G. Advertising and Promotion, 220
III. Financial Data, 221
    A. Proposal, 221
    B. Use of Proceeds, 221
    C. Opening Day Balance Sheet, 221
    D. Start-up Costs, 222
    E. Monthly Cash-Flow Projection, 224

Index   *227*

FOREWORD

Nearly all musicians dream of owning their own recording studio. I'm not talking about a porta-studio and a few outboard effects in a bedroom closet; I'm talking about an acoustically treated, isolated studio, with a separate control room and all the amenities. You know, Electric Ladyland in the basement. A couple of years ago, I got to thinking that with the new small-format multitracks and multi-effect DSPs, the whole concept was not so farfetched. For roughly the cost of an Acura Legend (loaded), any aging yuppie like myself could construct a pretty hot little "facility". All it takes is some time, effort and ingenuity.

I was wrong. Not about the cost—as it turned out, I could sell my Acura Legend and eke out the studio, costwise. I was wrong in that I underestimated the scope of the project in terms of design and complexity. Simply buying a bunch of recorders and outboard equipment does not constitute owning a recording studio. One must locate the equipment in a suitable area, design and implement a myriad of electronic connections, and learn to seriously understand the operation of the gear.

With a porta-studio, when you hear a ground buzz, you just rip off the ground pin on the offending device. You don't worry about clean technical grounds for hundreds of audio signal paths, balanced signal wire runs or separate line phases for lighting, power and audio. When you run out of outlets, you get a power tap. You don't have to upgrade your entire electrical service. When you're getting too much ambient noise, you throw a blanket over the whole setup. You don't get involved with STC 60 wall constructions and floating room designs. When the speakers sound boomy in your closet, you just pop the headphones on. You don't bother to consider Live End Dead End monitoring area constructions, standing wave elimination, diffusers or bass traps.

When I decided to build a real studio in my house, I began to get the sneaking suspicion that every physical law, every building code, and every economic system in existence was designed and put into place for the sole purpose of rendering the concept impractical. Part of this feeling arose from the fact that the information necessary to effectively build a working studio was not readily available.

I found books on acoustic theory that seemed to require a master's degree in physics to understand. I found books on construction and soundproofing that didn't really take into account the nuances of a recording studio situation. I found little or nothing about how to design a patch bay, make proper wiring connections, eliminate ground loops, configure a workable system, anticipate client needs, select compatible equipment, deal with dealers, etc.

Much of the practical information seemed to be milling about in the heads of various highly priced architectural engineers and megabuck electronic consultants who would have been happy to impart tidbits of information in exchange for exorbitant fees. These people provide invaluable services, no doubt, but they are not geared for the average Joe. Being just an average Joe, I chose instead the school of hard knocks.

I began my project studio after a plumbing defect destroyed most of my finished basement. I thought, since I have to rebuild the area from scratch, why not throw in some extra money and make it a dream-come-true? Of course, I made some modifications to insure that this type of disaster would not happen again.

I talked it over with my wife and sons. My sons, not being old enough to count to one, had little to say. My wife, being old enough to count to well over thirty thousand (which was the anticipated start-up cost) was skeptical, but she let me go ahead, figuring it might head off any mid-life crisis that might be brewing in the recesses of my brain. The result is what we call "Bon MarchC Productions" (Bon MarchC translates literally to "Good Market," but means "inexpensive" or "bargain")—a sixteen-track project studio with a full MIDI suite, a 32x8x16 console capable of sending 54 channels at mixdown, and an isolated studio with vocal booth.

Today, Bon MarchC Productions is operating at full steam, producing radio spots, TV soundtracks, industrials, and music demos. We have made many upgrades, all paid for by studio proceeds. (We've even installed a New England Digital Synclavier.) The dream is now a reality. This book was written in an attempt to provide anyone who is considering a project of this type with useful technical information and tips. You will still need to incorporate some trial and error, determination and luck, however, with the help of this book you should at least be aware of what's around every corner as you embark on your journey. I wish you success.

INTRODUCTION

We live in a new era of sound recording. It is now possible to generate crystal-clear, CD-quality, fully orchestrated stereo (and beyond) recordings within the confines of a domestic dwelling. The investment required to produce this kind of output is actually less than a tenth of what it cost to put together a moderately equipped professional recording studio only a decade ago. More importantly, it is within the financial grasp of a large percentage of individual hobbyists, artists, and small-scale recording professionals.

This fact is turning the recording industry upside down. Manufacturers of professional recording equipment are scrambling to fill a new market niche centered around the private artist. As a result, the development of low-cost, high-quality recording equipment is snowballing. Professional recording studios have had to revamp their business plans to take into account the fact that most small-scale recording projects (such as demos) are being done by the artists themselves in their homes.

From this point forward, I will use the term "studio" to mean "project studio" (or "home studio"), as opposed to professional studio (though differences between the project and pro studios are becoming less distinguishable with time).

Throughout this book I'll be discussing the equipment and constructional considerations necessary to build and operate a project recording studio. My intention is to assist those people who wish to go beyond the basic "bedroom studio" and enter the realm of professional or near-professional recording—though much of what is discussed can also be used or adapted to enhance the quality of the porta-studio environment.

I do not expect the reader to be a seasoned recording engineer, and I have deliberately avoided any highly technical discussions, mathematical formulas, or theory dissertations from the rocket-scientist school of recording practice. However, I must assume that the reader is reasonably familiar with the process of multitrack recording, as this is not a manual for those wishing to learn about this rather intricate art. I will take the time (where necessary) to go into certain specific aspects of recording, and offer information on new developments in the field of recording that are critical to the design and development of a studio.

ACKNOWLEDGMENTS

First and foremost, for her unending patience, understanding and support, which make any and all of my achievements possible, I thank my wife, Donna.

Next, I would like to thank the people in my life who, over the course of years (beginning with musical projects, leading to the construction of the studio, and culminating in this book), gave willingly of their hearts, minds, and talents, asking little or nothing in return.

For their dedication, hard work, and expertise, I thank my partners at Bon Marché, Mike Mullally and Wes Schroeppel. For his sheer musical prowess and collaborative efforts I thank Phil Sivilli. For always believing in me as a friend, I thank Mike Versaci. For walking with me along that fine line between normality and madness, and keeping me from wandering too far into either, I thank Tom Ryan, Jeri Cavagnaro and Peggy Price. For their direct and indirect assistance in the construction of the studio, I thank Sal Greco, Tom Ryan (again), Harry Pashkoff, Mike Maracello, Bill Savage, Bruce Elgort, Dan Virgilio, Jay Pickus, and Albert Costabile. For their invaluable technical support I thank Bob Muldowney, Larry Ketchell, and Robert Miller of Sam Ash Music, Prescott Jennings III, and Jeff Camp. For the photographique magnifique, I thank Francis Galluccio. For putting up with me through rough schedules, unfair demands, and moments of complete insanity, I thank my family, Mom, Dad, Nanny, Doug, and Anna.

This book is dedicated to my children, Dominick and Jordan—may your lives be filled with love and music.

Photo Credits

Figure 2.3 Tascam Portastudio, courtesy of TEAC America, Inc., all rights reserved.

Figure 2.4 Tascam TSR-8, courtesy of TEAC America, Inc., all rights reserved.

Figure 2.5 Tascam MSR-16, courtesy of TEAC America, Inc., all rights reserved.

Figure 2.6 Fostex R-8, courtesy of Fostex Corporation of America.

Figure 2.7 Fostex G-16, courtesy of Fostex Corporation of America.

Figure 2.8 Example screen from Vision sequencing program, courtesy of Opcode Systems, Inc.

Figure 2.9 MIDI Time Piece, courtesy of Mark Of The Unicorn, Inc.

Figure 2.10 Roland U-220 Sound Module, courtesy of Roland Corporation.

Figure 2.11 Akai S950 Sampler, courtesy of Akai.

Figure 2.12 Tascam Midiizer, courtesy of TEAC of America, Inc., all rights reserved.

Figure 2.13 TAC Scorpion II Console, courtesy of AMEK Corporation.

Figure 2.14 Tascam Rack Mount Mixers, courtesy of TEAC of America, Inc., all rights reserved.

Figure 2.15 Alesis Quadraverb, courtesy of Alesis Corporation.

Figure 2.16 Aphex Aural Exciter, courtesy of Aphex Systems.

Figure 2.17 Tascam DA-30 DAT, courtesy of TEAC of America, Inc., all rights reserved.

Figure 2.18 Korg Sound Link DAW, courtesy of Korg USA.

Figure 2.19 Roland DM-80 DAW, courtesy of Roland Corporation.

Figure 2.20 Alesis ADAT Digital 8-track Recorder, courtesy of Alesis Corporation.

Figure 2.21 Peavey PRM 3105 Monitors, courtesy of Peavey Electronics Corporation.

Figure 2.22 Yamaha NS-10M Monitors, courtesy of Yamaha Corporation of America.

Figure 2.23 Peavey PMA 200 Amplifier, courtesy of Peavey Electronics Corporation.

Figure 2.24 AKG 414, courtesy of AKG Acoustics, Inc.

Figure 2.25 Sennheiser 421, courtesy of Sennheiser.

Figure 2.26 Shure SM-57, courtesy of Shure Brothers Incorporated.

Figure 5.1 Furman PB-40 Patchbay, courtesy of Furman, Inc.

Figure 5.4 Furman Power Conditioner, courtesy of Furman, Inc.

Figure 7.3 RPG Diffusor, courtesy of RPG Systems, Inc.

Figure 7.4 ART Diffusor, courtesy of Systems Development Group.

THE DESIGN PROCESS: GETTING IT DOWN ON PAPER

If you're interested in building a project recording studio, you should ask yourself, "What is a recording studio?" This may seem like a strange question, but there are different answers that come to mind depending on the type of person that you are and the work that you do. Here are some examples:

- A recording studio is a facility designed to faithfully capture voice or musical performances onto a reproducible medium.

- A recording studio is a facility that can enhance the quality of sound, and impart a creative aspect to audio performances not possible in live listening situations.

- A recording studio is a sexy-looking room with lots of neat equipment, faders, buttons, meters, blinking lights, incredible sounding speakers, and plenty of sound effects.

All three answers are correct and are attitudes you can expect to encounter in a recording studio. Some artists will ask you to provide a perfectly transparent replication of the natural sound of an instrument or group–a tall order for any recording engineer. Some will play the studio like an instrument, using it to impart new expression to the work. And some book studio time to impress themselves and their friends, have a good time for a few hours, and walk out with a tape that, if they're lucky, sounds about as good as they hoped for.

Be honest with yourself and try to establish what your idea of a recording studio is. What is it that you hope to accomplish? Do you record mostly electronic instruments, or do you need a natural-sounding room for acoustic instruments? Are esthetics important?

If the studio you're building is intended strictly for your own personal use, you'll be able to tailor your setup to do precisely what you need. Otherwise, you'll need to design a facility that can accommodate all the personality types you'll encounter.

You may wish to specialize in some way–concentrating on video postproduction and audio sampling, for example. This will certainly have a profound effect on the layout of your studio and the equipment you'll need.

The amount of care and time that you take in designing your studio, before any purchases or construction, will be a deciding factor in the ultimate success of the project. You shouldn't lift a finger in that soon-to-be-a-studio area until you have finalized every aspect of the equipment list, financing plans, studio layout, construction materials and outside services (if any). Spend a lot of time talking to people about your project– friends, musicians, local merchants and salespersons. Subscribe to related magazines, and try to keep up-to-date on new developments in the audio field. This is not an overnight endeavor; you must take your time.

The Business of Recording

A word to the wise for those who are considering using their home studios as a business: There is more to running a business than simply putting an ad in the local music paper and charging money. As a business owner, you'll be required to register with your local government office, declare income and pay taxes, collect sales tax (where applicable), keep accurate records, and comply with the labor laws in your state. If you decide to sell recording time to the general public, you'll be letting strangers into your home on a regular basis. You must decide how to handle various booking situations, cancellations, no-shows, methods of payment, and a host of other potentially sticky situations. Finally, be prepared to find yourself sitting behind the board at three in the morning listening to the Screaming Voidoids From Hell laying down the fortieth take of chorus vocals for their song "I Love You, Baby, but You Stink Like a Pig. "

The rewards, however, are many. If you are successful, you will be taking an active role in the production of many different musical works, and it is likely that you will come in contact with some incredible musicians. You may become involved in video or film projects, or hook up with a record company to record demos for their new and upcoming bands. Working in an area where creativity and technology are both paramount is an unusual and exciting situation.

For those of you brave enough and ambitious enough to do it, I have included a chapter at the end of this book with some tips on running the day-to-day aspects of the business. Even if you're just using your studio for personal use, there are some discussions in that chapter about zoning, taxes, and record keeping that are important to any studio owner.

A Caution About Zoning

Many residential zoning laws prohibit the use of homes for commercial business. The primary reason for zoning laws is that people do not want their quiet neighborhoods turned into commercial areas with clients coming and going at all hours, cars parked up and down the street, people milling about outside, and so on. Zoning laws also require that commercial businesses offering public access meet strict building codes dealing with parking, access for the handicapped, fire prevention, safety features and other considerations that the average home studio owner might not be in a position to provide.

There is a great deal of controversy surrounding the issue of home studios being used for commercial purposes. The owners of professional recording studios argue that home studios are competing unfairly because they do not incur the same expenses associated with building codes in commercial areas. This may be a legitimate gripe. Beware: If you are operating a home studio in an area that is not zoned for it, and you are advertising studio time to the general public, you may find a local building inspector at your door acting on a complaint from a commercial studio in town. If the inspector finds that you are indeed operating in violation of the law, you will be ordered to cease operation.

You may apply for a zoning variance (an exception to the zoning rule based on special circumstances). This involves a local hearing of the zoning board, of which all of your neighbors living within a certain radius of your home will be notified and given the opportunity to support or reject your request for variance. It is recommended that you hire a lawyer if you decide to apply for a zoning variance.

Home studio owners argue that the line between commercial use and private use of a studio is not clearly defined. If you use your home studio only to write and produce your own music, you are operating legally. However, if that music ends up being sold commercially (for example, if it becomes a hit record), you are technically in violation of most residential zoning laws. Home studio proponents also point out that federal tax laws have been set up to promote the use of the home for business purposes through tax breaks, but many zoning laws conflict with this.

Whichever side of this issue you sympathize with, be sure to clarify your particular situation before going ahead with a commercial business venture.

The Range of Possibilities

The project studio can be anything you want it to be within your personal resources. There are "home studios" that incorporate millions of dollars worth of equipment and design. The only thing that sets them apart from high-end professional studios is the fact that they exist in someone's residence. We will not be discussing that extreme in this book.

For the purposes of illustration throughout the text, I will be referring to two different designs:

- Studio A—a minimal yet effective single-room 8-track studio
- Studio B—a 16-track setup representing a more substantial effort and investment, capable of operating as a commercial facility

Studio A can be constructed on a budget of roughly $10,000, while Studio B is based on an actual design that cost $40,000 to implement. These are intended only as examples, and there are a host of other possible designs.

Studio B is the studio that I built in my home (Bon Marche´ Productions), so I will be using it as an example of this type of setup. However, this type of studio could easily be a project studio in a commercial building, or even a private project studio for a business.

Use of Space

The first task is to carefully map out the available space for the studio. The size and shape of the space will determine the type of equipment that can be used and the scope of the work that can take place there. If there will be changes to the existing room configuration, keep in mind that it is difficult and potentially expensive to move supporting walls, electrical service boxes, and large heating fixtures (especially furnaces or coal-burning stoves). Nonsupporting walls, electrical outlets and radiant heating fixtures can usually be removed or relocated with relative ease.

Most professional studios are divided into two distinct areas by an isolating wall (see Figure 1.1). The bulk of the recording equipment is located on the control room side of the wall. The room opposite is known as the studio or talent room. Ideally, the two rooms are completely isolated from each other in terms of sound transmission. The reason for this is that the recording engineer must hear only those sounds that are coming through the monitor speakers and not the live sound that is being generated in the studio.

For example, when a drummer plays in the studio, the sound from the drums is picked up by a series of microphones, which alter the natural sound of the drums. The sound is again modified as it passes through the mixing board and may be processed even further by the addition of equalization and effects. Finally, this processed sound is sent to the monitor speakers and to the input of the tape deck. If the engineer is listening to the monitor speakers and can also hear sound coming from the drum set itself, his or her perception of what is actually going down on tape will be false.

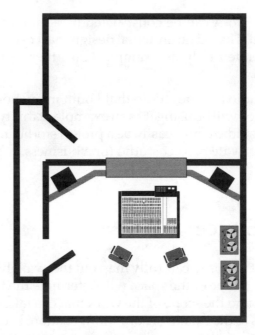

Figure 1.1   A typical two-room studio floor plan.

With some extra effort and know-how, it is possible to make good recordings of live instruments without an isolated studio/control room layout. Your budget and the available space will determine whether you can afford the luxury of an isolated room. It's also not necessary to locate the studio in an area adjacent to the control room. It might involve some tricky wire routing, but the two can be several rooms apart, and the engineer can communicate with the talent via an audio or audio/visual communications link.

The trend in recent years is to devote more space to the control room and less to the studio area, a reversal from traditional recording studios, which often featured tiny control rooms. One reason for this trend is that more and more instruments are being recorded "direct," that is, without the use of an acoustic microphone. Electronic synthesizers can plug directly into the mixer. Drum machines and sequencers often take the place of a live acoustic drum set. Recent developments in speaker emulation have resulted in amplifier simulators that an electric guitarist can use to plug directly into the board and still achieve an authentic guitar amp sound. For bass guitars, where speaker emulation is less critical, the instrument can be plugged in through a simple "direct box," which converts the low level signal from the bass into a higher level signal that can be processed by the mixer.

Using these methods, a typical rock band can be recorded using a microphone only for vocals. (They still haven't figured out a way to plug your vocal cords into a line input—give them time.) If this is the only type of recording you anticipate, a separate room may not be necessary.

Another reason for the trend towards large control rooms is that many studios are being used as media rooms. These are facilities designed to work with both audio and video. In that case, the control room must be large enough to comfortably seat a production team as well as an engineering staff, and it must afford a suitable viewing space for all involved. If your goal is to record soundtracks for film or video, TV commercials, jingles, animation, and so on, you'll need to take this into consideration when laying out the control room. The mixing console will, of course, be located directly in front of the TV and audio monitors. However, behind the console, a small table or "producer's desk" is set up to provide a work surface for the producers, while keeping them within the stereo image of the monitor speakers.

Planning Your Space

This section is an overview of what to take into account when planning your studio space. Here, I list only the concepts. The mechanics of each are discussed in detail in later chapters.

Access

Consider who will be entering and leaving the studio. Will musicians be lugging drum kits and amplifier stacks in and out on a regular basis? If so, how many flights of stairs will they have to go up or down? Will they be entering the house through the living room or kitchen, wreaking daily havoc on the poor unfortunate people who happen to live there? If the studio will be used commercially, a separate entrance is almost mandatory. In my home studio, there is an outside entrance to the basement at the rear of the house, and another from the main floor, both at the top of the stairs. The indoor entrance was bolted shut to keep clients from entering the private area of the house.

Soundproofing

If you prefer to monitor at high SPLs (Sound Pressure Levels–a measure of loudness) or if you'll be recording screaming guitar amps and killer drums, you must take steps to avoid disrupting others in the house and/or the surrounding neighborhood. Similarly, it is undesirable to have outside noises such as traffic, footsteps or loud voices filtering into the studio while recording or monitoring. Therefore, the space must be treated acoustically to keep studio sound in and lock outside sound out. Unfortunately, such treatment will invariably take up space, of which most home studios have precious little to begin with.

If the studio space is located in a basement with concrete walls and floor, the main area of concern will be with ceiling treatment and any outside windows. In this ideal situation, it is not necessary to factor in a lot of space for soundproofing materials. Beware, though, of noisy, motor-driven devices that tend to lurk in basements, especially furnaces or central vacuuming units. These horrible machines transmit low-frequency shudders through walls and floors that will disrupt the recording process. Effectively isolating these monsters can sometimes be expensive. If you are stricken with one of these afflictions, the easiest and cheapest way to combat it may be simply to shut the thing off every time you begin a session.

On a main or upper-level floor, the acoustic separation between the studio and the rest of the world is likely to be weaker. It may be necessary to sacrifice up to a foot of space along each wall to achieve even a moderately effective sound barrier. Chapter 3 deals with the methods of soundproofing that can be used, and will give you an accurate idea of the amount of space needed to implement them.

In some cases it may be necessary to incorporate a sound lock, which is an air space between the control room exit and the studio entrance. The sound lock is also described in Chapter 3.

Wire Routing

A moderately equipped recording studio may contain more than two miles of signal wire. The last place you want two miles of wire is along the floor of your workspace. The obvious reasons are it's a nuisance and it looks horrible; but the most important reason is the wire will be subject to mechanical abuse if it's left out in the workplace. People will step on it, get it caught in their clothing, pull on it, and so on. Only jacketed cable (guitar cord and the like) is built to withstand limited mechanical abuse, and unless you've recently won the lottery, you can't afford two miles of jacketed cable. Consequently, you must plan to route signal wire within the walls, ceilings, and furniture or beneath the floor of your studio.

Most professional studios are built on raised floors, with removable panels allowing service access to the wiring troughs located beneath them. Few home studios have the ceiling height required to achieve this design, so you'll have to be creative. Rack-mounting equipment right into a wall is one way to hide wiring (but make sure you have access to the rear of the equipment). Another is to mount equipment into cabinets that have internal space for wiring. Both of these methods were used in Studio B, and the details for these designs will be presented in later chapters.

Maintenance Access

One of the mistakes I made when building my studio was not allowing for easy access to the rear of some of my rack-mounted equipment. It's not impossible to reach, it's just that on one of my racks, I have to go through some nasty contortions every time I need to unplug an audio input or wire something into the rear of the patchbay. This has turned out to be more than just an annoyance. Never underestimate the amount of times you need to get to the back of a unit. There is no one piece of equipment in the studio for which you can say, "I'll hardly ever need to get behind that."

When building equipment into a wall, make sure that it is either very easily removed or that you open a passageway behind it large enough for you to move in and have elbow room. One really good but difficult solution is to design a hinge that enables the rack to swing out from the wall. Don't forget when making connections to use several extra feet of wire at that point to allow for the movement of the rack. Also, if you build equipment into a cabinet, be sure to include doors at the rear of the cabinet large enough for you to comfortably reach the output jacks on your machines.

Finally, leave room between the mixing console and the wall–chances are you'll be spending a lot of time there.

Acoustics

Sometimes, a separate studio with finely tuned room acoustics is used to impart sonically pleasant enhancements to the instrument sounds. Studios will advertise things like "the best-sounding drum room in L.A." A truly superior acoustic space never happens by accident. It requires some sophisticated design engineering, the proper space and materials, and often a great deal of expense to create. Some acoustic engineers are of the opinion that if any room dimension is less than 10 feet, or if the volume of space is less than 1500 cubic feet, there is no point in trying to create a superior acoustic space. While this level of performance is usually beyond the scope of the home studio, it is possible to design a small acoustic space for recording that will provide reasonably good sound.

When planning the control room or monitoring area, it is important that the area be properly designed from an acoustic standpoint. Monitoring in a poor acoustical area actually will cause you to adjust the sound you hear in such a way as to make it worse. For example, if the room geometry tends to de-emphasize low frequencies, you'll be hearing very little bass as you mix. This will cause you to boost the bass frequencies until they sound "right" to you. Later, when you listen to the tape on another system, you may find that your violin concerto sounds like a tuba fest. What you want in your control room is an acoustically neutral monitoring area. You don't want an acoustically "dead" room. Hanging up rugs, foam and egg cartons all over your control room will simply absorb all the high frequencies, leaving you again to mix in a false environment.

Chapter 5 gives some guidance as to how to create a reasonably good monitoring area. Since much depends on the shape of the room itself, it is necessary to have a design in mind while planning your space.

Equipment Layout and Ergonomics

Your recording equipment will take up most of the space in the control room. The object is to locate the equipment where it allows functional operator access, relatively easy service access, and effective work surfaces, while maintaining a certain degree of operator comfort. This is known as ergonomic designing. But that's not all you have to think about. You also have to make sure that the monitors are properly located in relation to the operator or engineer while operating the equipment, and if you're really serious, you should consider how the equipment layout will affect the acoustic situation in the room.

If you anticipate recording alone, functioning as both talent and engineer, you'll have to take special precautions when designing your layout to insure that you have access to all necessary recording functions while you are playing the instruments.

Heating, Ventilation and Air Conditioning

Depending on the climate you live in, you'll have to provide a varying degree of climate control. Ductwork for air heat and air conditioning takes up considerable space, and the location of the systems is critical from the standpoint of noise reduction. The quietest form of air conditioning is a stand-alone motor/compressor system that can be located outside the studio area, with ductwork built into ceilings to transfer cool air into the room. If your budget allows, you can also install special dampers into the ductwork to diffuse the air flow, cutting down further on noise. In my studio, there was not enough ceiling space to install ductwork, so I ended up using discrete air-conditioning units built into the window areas. In summer, we run the units for several hours before a session to cool down the rooms, then turn them off while taping. (Yes, this is a hassle, but I had the foresight to install a special switch near the console for this purpose.) The control-room unit is a newer model featuring a fairly quiet compressor. It is necessary only to shut it down occasionally to monitor quiet passages or pick out fine nuances in the mix.

Isolation Booth

It is usually desirable to record musical instruments in a live acoustic space. However, it may be beneficial to do some things such as voice-overs; and, in some cases, guitars, percussion, and wind instruments in a dead space where there are no acoustical reflections at all. For this purpose you might want to build an isolation booth.

It is not necessary to soundproof the walls of the isolation booth unless you intend to use the room to completely isolate instruments during live sessions. The main concern is to acoustically treat the inside surfaces to eliminate reflections. See Chapter 5 for details.

Plumbing

For those of you who plan to sell studio time, your clients will need access to rest-room facilities. If there is no bathroom in the studio area, and you don't want strange people traipsing through the rest of your house, you must install a bathroom. This requires a building permit and may affect your property taxes.

Workspace Examples

The following are some examples intended to give you an idea of the considerations necessary when planning the workspace. The configurations shown represent just a few of the myriad possibilities in any situation.

Figure 1.2 is a diagram of a small space available for Studio A. Working with this diagram, which includes room dimensions and prominent room features such as doors, windows, electrical outlets, and so on; I developed a typical, single-room setup with outboard effects, mixdown deck, power amps, and mixer, mounted in a vertical equipment rack. This is an extremely efficient use of space.

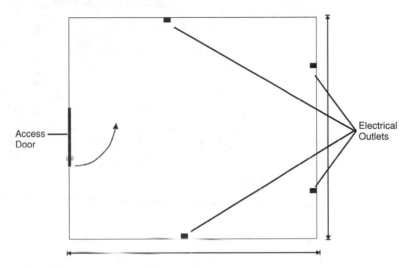

Figure 1.2   The dimensions of a small room.

Figure 1.3 shows one layout approach, with the equipment rack and the analog multitrack on either side of the workstation. The operator faces the short wall across from the door. Although it is nicely symmetrical, there are some problems with this layout. First, the operator will soon tire of wheeling back and forth from the multitrack to the equipment rack. Also, the mixer inputs are at the opposite end of the room from the multitrack; you would require a 12-foot snake (a potentially expensive multiwire cable) to connect them.

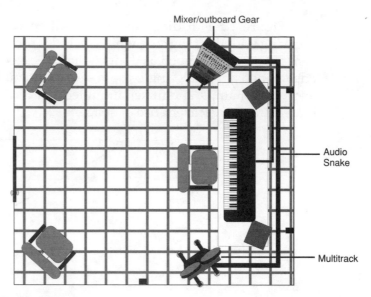

Figure 1.3 The first layout.

Figure 1.4 shows a better solution. The orientation of the components allows the operator to use nearly all the equipment with minimal movement. Also, the mixer inputs are right next to the multitrack, cutting down on snake length.

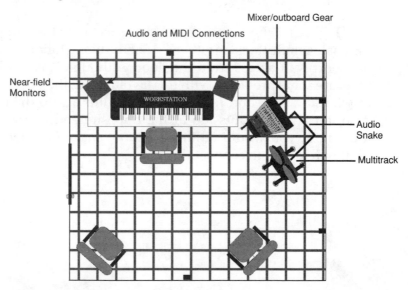

Figure 1.4 The layout of a small studio.

Now take a look at a larger space, into which Studio B will be built. In this example, the available space was a basement in a 60-year-old house. Figure 1.5 shows the original form of the basement with existing walls and permanent and semipermanent structures. My first step was to mentally gut the area, removing all temporary structures. Then I drew some possible layouts for a control room, MIDI area, talent area and isolation booth.

Figures 1.6 and 1.7 show two early ideas for converting the original space. In Figure 1.6, I considered locating the control room in the center, facing an elongated studio area. This proved to be unsuitable because of awkward access to the control room, and because such a large talent area wasted space.

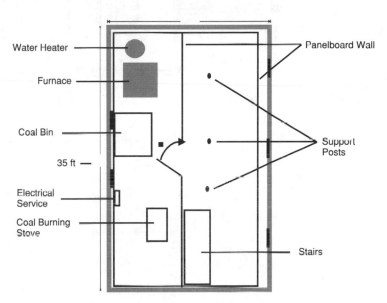

Figure 1.5 The original basement.

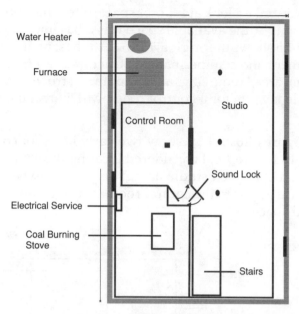

Figure 1.6 The first design, with a central control room facing the studio.

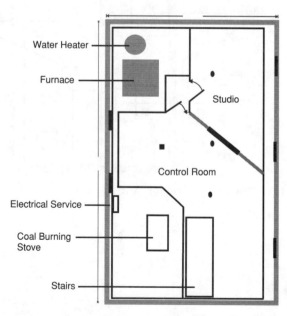

Figure 1.7 An early design with a V-shaped central control room.

In Figure 1.7, I tried to skew the control room wall, giving me a longer wall surface for a larger window and more room on each side of the board, while at the same time using a large amount of the space to create a V-shaped control room. This might have worked out well (also from an acoustic standpoint) except for the fact that there were several unmovable structures in the way, one of which was right where I wanted to put the console.

I finally decided upon the layout shown in Figure 1.8 as the best design in terms of use of space, functionality, and ease of construction. The control room takes up most of the space in the overall layout. The alcove to the left provides a space for the open-reel tape machines (keeping them away from people who tend to lean on anything, even if it's moving). The machines are controlled through remote units located at the console. (If you were paying attention to the previous example for Studio A, you might ask, "What about snake length?" Good question—I cut down on the cost of a multiline snake by using discrete wiring run through the ceiling. Chapter 4 explains this in detail.)

Note that the right-hand wall was built three feet out from the foundation wall, allowing the installation of flush-mounted equipment racks and patchbay wiring. One foot of space was allocated to the double-studded isolation wall between the control room and the talent area. The talent area became nearly square in dimension (an acoustical no-no), but the introduction of the isolation booth with its angled walls broke up some of the parallel surfaces. A sound lock was installed between the control room and the studio to maintain double-wall isolation.

Most outboard equipment was mounted in a cabinet behind the console (see Figure 1.9), allowing easy access for the engineers. The cabinet doubles as the controller keyboard stand and computer desk. All signal wiring is routed into the cabinet, and then into the wall to the patchbay area.

Luckily, there is a private entrance to the cellar. Because of the design of my house, it was possible to allow access to a rest-room facility on the main floor while keeping the rest of the house closed to studio traffic. Keeping part of the space closed off as a storage area has proven to be of enormous benefit over time.

These designs are presented as suggestions to give you an idea of the kind of thinking that goes into planning how to use space. To come up with the optimum configuration, experiment and be creative with the space you have available.

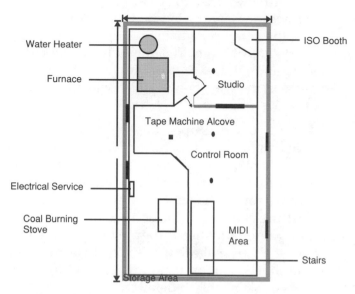

Water Heater

Furnace

Tape Machine Alcove

Electrical Service

Coal Burning
Stove

ISO Booth

Studio

Control Room

MIDI
Area

Stairs

Storage Area

Figure 1.8   The final design.

Figure 1.9   The front of the cabinet.

A Final Note

As you get further into the design process, it will become evident that all these concerns are interrelated, and changes in one aspect will usually affect all of the other aspects in some way. Through effective planning and design, the resulting studio will function like a well-oiled machine. It will be comfortable, serviceable, expandable and, most of all, functional in the areas that your needs dictate. When all is said and done, it is the output of the studio that will be the yardstick by which you measure success. Recordings will be your end product, and although the equipment plays a large part in the quality of the recordings, the ability of the studio to function as a creative environment may be just as critical.

STUDIO EQUIPMENT: MAKING THE RIGHT DECISIONS

In this chapter, I'll cover the types of equipment available and the things a studio builder should take into account when specifying equipment. Choosing equipment is also part of the design process, and if there will be any construction work as part of your studio, it helps to know exactly which products you are going to use before beginning this work. Before going into the specific types of equipment, there are three overall concerns that I will discuss, and these apply to all equipment decisions: compatibility, state-of-the-art, and the recording process. If you don't understand some of the terms presented, don't worry. The technical aspects of the equipment will be explained in the sections detailing the different types of equipment.

Compatibility

For every audio product that you intend to use, you must determine its ability to interface with the rest of your equipment. This should be your first priority. Even two pieces of equipment purchased from the same manufacturer may not be compatible in terms of signal level or software protocol.

Most audio equipment is designed and calibrated to operate at a specific signal level. There are several possible types of signal level; however, the most prevalent are Mike and Line levels. These designations have to do with the strength of the signal that the device intends to receive or deliver and the impedance of the associated inputs and outputs. The pickup coils of an electric guitar produce an output of roughly –20db, which is a very weak signal. Guitar amplifiers are built to take such input and amplify it accordingly. A Line-level mixer input, however, is intended for signals of approximately –10db to +4db level. Since every 3db represents a doubling of signal strength, a guitar output is three times weaker than Line level. If you plug a guitar output directly into the mixer input, you'll find that in order to bring the signal to a reasonable level, you'll have to run the mixer input wide open and the volume fader cranked to the maximum. This will amplify not only the guitar signal but any ambient noise in the signal. It also leaves you with no *headroom* whatsoever (headroom is the range of signal level that can be recorded onto the tape without saturating at the high end or being drowned out by hiss on the low end). To remedy this, the guitar signal must be sent to a preamplifier where it will be boosted to Line level, and then connected to the board. Mike inputs are more sensitive. If you plug a Line level signal into a Mike level input, you overload the input, causing distortion and again limiting headroom.

The bottom line is that you can't connect a Line output to a Mike input or vice versa without compromising the quality of the audio signal. This incompatibility is very often found between tape machines and mixers. Most home studio and semiprofessional mixers can accept signals of either level at the channel inputs, but tape sends and returns usually work on just one of those levels. You need to make sure that the tape deck sends and receives the same levels. There are line transformers that can convert signals from one level to another; however, they cost upwards of $20 apiece, and if you have a multitrack tape deck with 16 inputs and 16 outputs, you'll need 32 transformers.

Connections to an audio device can be balanced or unbalanced. Unbalanced connections are found in most of the less expensive equipment, and require only two wires feeding into the connector: one signal connection and one ground connection. The connector can be a quarter-inch mono jack or an RCA plug. For balanced connections, there are two signal wires and a ground wire. Balanced wires are terminated either by XLR-type connectors or quarter-inch stereo plugs. Balanced wiring is less subject to noise interference and can also be run longer than unbalanced wire without significant high-frequency drop-off. Figure 2.1 shows some typical connectors. These will be discussed further in Chapters 5 and 6.

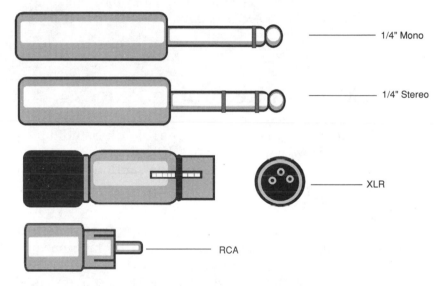

1/4" Mono

1/4" Stereo

XLR

RCA

Figure 2.1 Different types of connectors.

The State of the Art

Recording equipment technology is changing so rapidly that writing an up-to-date book on this subject is like trying to board a moving train. The best way to stay current with technology is to attend trade shows or conventions such as those organized by the Audio Engineering Society (AES), the National Association of Musical Equipment Manufacturers

(NAMM), and the Society of Motion Picture and Television Engineers (SMPTE). Most of these conventions take place once a year in major cities around the country, and feature demonstrations of the newest equipment from all the top manufacturers.

Since most people don't have a travel budget that allows them to attend all of these prestigious events, it's necessary to keep abreast of technology through trade publications. I've listed the most widely read ones in Appendix A. Almost all of these offer equipment reviews each month. Talking with local music retailers is often helpful, but you'll sometimes encounter salespeople promoting whatever line of equipment they need to move that month, and they may not always provide you with an unbiased or objective discussion of the products.

The Modern Recording Process

Mention to anyone that you have a recording studio and you are invariably asked, "How many tracks is it?" If the intent is to determine the capabilities of the recording studio, the question is no longer valid in today's world. It's like trying to determine how fast a car can go by asking how many cylinders it has.

Tradition requires that you answer the dreaded question by stating the number of tracks on your largest analog tape machine. Therefore, if you use an 8-track analog recorder, you would dutifully reply, "It's an 8-track recording studio." However, with MIDI sequencers, digital disk-based recorders, submixers, samplers, synchronizers and other devices lurking about, the number of simultaneous channels available for sound processing (especially at mixdown) may be literally into the hundreds. A well-designed "8-track" studio could have more recording "horsepower" than a poorly equipped 24-track facility. The implication that projects recorded in 24-track studios generally sound better than those recorded in 8- or 16-track studios is just not true. If it were, someone with a good ear would theoretically be capable of determining many tracks were used by listening to the quality of a recording, and I have yet to meet anyone who can.

Take a look at the modern recording process to see what really constitutes recording capability.

Figure 2.2 is a block diagram of the typical components found in today's recording studio. To make a recording (a song, for argument's sake), a number of musical sounds are generated and saved on various formats. Analog sounds, such as guitars and vocals, are recorded onto different tracks of the analog multitrack tape machine. MIDI messages controlling digital sound generators are saved to computer memory via a sequencing software program. These are called "virtual tracks" and could account for the keyboard sounds, bass sounds and electronic drum sounds. Background vocals might recorded on a two-track recorder or sampled into a sampler. Or, better yet, they could be sampled onto a hard disk digital recording system, and played back where needed via a keyboard controller or MIDI message from the computer (this is known as "flying in" the background vocals).

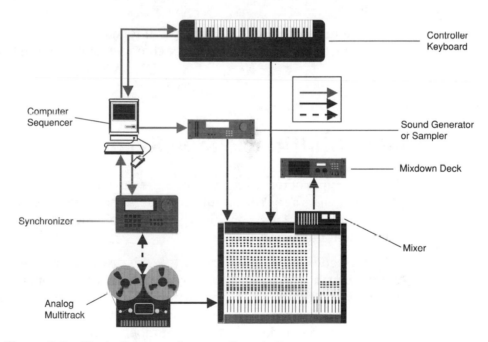

Figure 2.2 Block diagram of a recording studio.

One of these many machines is then designated as the *master*, and all the other machines become *slaves*, locking themselves to the time code of the master through the synchronizer. As soon as you tell the master to "play," the slaves obediently play along, in perfect synchronization (hopefully) with the master and each other. The result is a potentially enormous number of sounds funnelling into the mixing console. The operator of this beast then takes all the different sounds from all the different sources, adjusts their relative sound levels, adds equalization and effects to taste, pans each one a clever amount to the left, right or center, and routes the composite signal through the stereo bus to the mixdown recorder. The result is a completed master tape.

As you can see, the number of tracks the studio boasts has little to do with the complexity of the production that it can handle and even less to do with the sound quality of the finished tape. By far the most important factors contributing to the outcome of any recording are the time and care put into production, and the knowledge and expertise of the artists and engineers.

The remainder of this chapter will focus on the major components, discussing the features, performance characteristics and relative prices for each.

Analog Multitrack Tape Recorders

For most types of recording, you need fewer analog tracks today than you did a few years ago. You should consider what priority should be placed on the multitrack tape machine when allocating money in your budget for equipment purchases.

Cassette-format multitracks (see Figure 2.3) are inexpensive and convenient; however, the superior sound quality of an open-reel machine is easily discernible in all but a few cases. Also, in the case of most *portastudios* (multitrack cassette recorders with built-in mixers), the mixer section may be inadequate for the number of inputs you'll find yourself using if you tie in a MIDI sequencer. Many of the newer portastudios have taken this into account and added additional mixer inputs for MIDI users.

Despite the limitations of cassette multitracks, be cautious about spending a large amount of money on an open-reel 16-, 24-, or (gulp) 32-track tape deck. Also, as the number of tracks on your analog tape deck grows, so too will the tape width. While most 8-track decks use 1/4-inch,

1/2-inch or 1-inch tape, most 24-track machines use 2-inch tape (although there are now some low-cost 24-track decks that operate on a 1-inch format). Even if you buy it in bulk, a 2,500 foot reel of 2-inch tape costs well over $100, and at 30 inches per second, that one reel will give you only about 16 minutes of recording time.

Figure 2.3 Tascam portastudio.

Beware of used multitrack tape machines. The multitrack is the one piece of studio gear that requires the most maintenance. It has more moving parts than almost anything else in the studio, and it will probably be subjected to the most use and consequent wear and tear on heads, capstans, and motors. This stuff is not generally cheap to replace, and upkeep on an old multitrack can get expensive. Unless you are very good at electronics and can do your own repairs and maintenance on the machine, a used multitrack deck is not recommended.

The best choice of analog deck for a home studio is one of the new small-format (1/2-inch, 8- or 16-track reel-to-reel machines, such as the Tascam TSR-8 (see Figure 2.4) or MSR-16 (see Figure 2.5) and the Fostex R8 and G16 (see Figures 2.6 and 2.7). These machines were specifically designed for the home studio market. They are moderately priced (probably less than a used professional large format 8- or 16-track), and they contain many new features that older professional machines lack (and would require expensive add-on equipment to duplicate).

Figure 2.4   Tascam 8-track.

Figure 2.5   Tascam 16-track.

For example, both the Fostex and the Tascam machines have built-in noise reduction systems. The Tascam uses dbx and the Fostex uses Dolby S. Both types of noise reduction reduce tape hiss on these machines to negligible levels, and they increase headroom considerably. To add outboard noise reduction to a multitrack machine that does not have its own built-in system will costs $50 to $100 *per track*.

Figure 2.6 Fostex 8-track.

Figure 2.7   Fostex 16-track.

Both the Fostex and Tascam machines also have synchronous control circuits, which means that the speed of the tape can be controlled by an external source. This is an incredible asset and allows you to synchronize your analog tape tracks to computer-generated sequencer tracks, video-tape time code, and many other master/slave timing devices (see "Synchronizers," later in this chapter). Additional standard features include multiple autolocate points, gapless punch-in and punch-out, and automatic punch-in and punch-out.

As for the sound quality of these machines, take a look into the number of megahit records that have been recorded on them recently

(M. C. Hammer's platinum album "Please Hammer, Don't Hurt 'Em" was recorded on an MSR-16).

Professional tape machines are invariably 2-inch format. If you are going to be jumping from studio to studio, or city to city, a 2-inch 24-track machine (such as the Otari MX-80) may pay off.

MIDI Sequencing Equipment

The next equipment group on the block diagram is the MIDI sequencing equipment. A brief reminder of how MIDI (Musical Instrument Digital Interface) works: You play a bunch of notes on an electronic keyboard (called the controller). A computer program records all the relevant information about the notes, for example, note on-time, note off-time, velocity (how hard you hit the note), and location (which key). The computer can now play the keyboard back exactly the way you played it by sending the information back to the synthesizer's internal sound generators. Or, it can play a different keyboard or bank of several keyboards and sound generators with that same information. This is called sequencing, as is the software designed to do it. Sequencing software also allows you to edit every parameter of the note information. You can add and subtract notes, change the tempo, pitch, duration, loudness, timing, and so on for any of the notes you played.

The computer may be built into the keyboard itself, housed in a free-standing device (sequencer), or it may be a separate microcomputer, such as a Macintosh or an IBM PC with sequencing software installed on a disk drive. Figure 2.8 shows a popular sequencing program loaded on a Macintosh. Most sequencers can record information for hundreds of tracks of music, and with a single sequencer, the only limitation on the number of instruments that can be played by the computer at one time is the number of sound generators you have that can understand MIDI information.

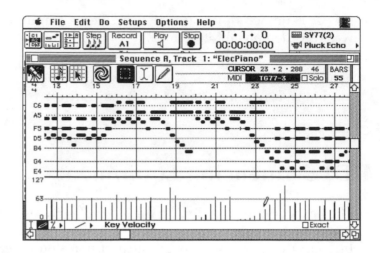

Figure 2.8 A screen from the Vision sequencing program.

Some small production studios are made up entirely of MIDI sound generators, sequenced and routed to a mixer, with no analog multitrack tape equipment at all. These "MIDI Suites" are perfectly capable of handling all the composition and arrangement (known as preproduction) for commercials, soundtracks, or industrials. After the music is sequenced, it is brought into the more expensive, full-service studio environment where vocals, acoustic instruments or other final touches are added.

There are two relatively inexpensive ways to set up for MIDI implementation. The first is to purchase a multiple-voice MIDI-compatible keyboard/sound generator, such as the Kawai K4 or the Roland D-2, and a simple stand-alone sequencer such as the Alesis MMT-8 or the Roland MC-50. This can be done for under $1000. The second is to purchase a *workstation*. MIDI workstations are keyboards with on-board sequencing programs and multiple voice sound generators, all built into a single machine. They range in price from $1200 to over $3000. Reasonably good workstations are being manufactured by Korg, Ensoniq, Roland, Yamaha, and Kurzweil.

While these are excellent tools for the songwriter, studio owners may find drawbacks to relying on a single workstation or a small, separate sequencer for MIDI applications. The memory capability of a small microprocessor housed in a keyboard workstation is limited compared to that of a computer; therefore, the number of tracks available and the length of the song(s) that can be played into the workstation sequencer might be limited.

Also, you are able to use only the sequencing software provided with the machine, which in most cases does not approach the level of sophistication of sequencing software available for computers. Having software flexibility also attracts clients who may wish to do their MIDI work at home or at other studios, and then bring the finished product to your studio for final production. Finally, nothing approaches the ease of operation of a software program that uses a computer screen to display MIDI information.

Higher priced stand-alone sequencers such as the Roland MKS-500 have adequate memory capability and more sophisticated software than the on-board workstation sequencers; however, they are not flexible in terms of sequencing software, and they do not use computer screens for editing. Their main advantage lies in their portability.

Possibly the best all-around sequencing machine is the Macintosh computer. Two of the most popular and sophisticated sequencing software programs, Vision and Performer, were written for the Macintosh because of its unique system architecture, which lends itself to the processing of MIDI information. Of course, it is also the most expensive. Other excellent sequencing programs are available for the IBM PC, the Atari ST, and the Commodore Amiga computers. Since more than 50% of all professional studios use the Macintosh, it may be worth it to spend the extra money on the Mac if you intend to interface with them.

To do any serious sequencing, the computer should be configured with a hard drive, a 3.5-inch high-density floppy drive and a minimum 1 M (preferably 2 M or more) of internal memory (RAM). For most computers, you'll also have to purchase an interface to connect the computer to outside MIDI devices, although there are a few with built-in MIDI ports. Interfaces range from extremely simple to extremely complex. The simplest interface is a box which allows connection to the computer modem or printer port on one side, and has two 5-pin MIDI connectors (one In, one Out) on the other side. These simple devices can actually handle quite a good-sized MIDI setup; however, if you daisy-chain many different MIDI machines, you may begin to experience a time delay between the note sent from the computer and the note information received by the last device in the chain. At this point, you need to upgrade to an interface that features several parallel MIDI output jacks.

Aside from providing MIDI connections, more sophisticated interfaces, such as the MIDI Time Piece by Mark of the Unicorn (see Figure 2.9) and Studio 5 by Opcode, perform additional useful MIDI functions such as internal routing functions, time-code read-and-write, and even MIDI effects such as time delay, compression, and expansion.

Figure 2.9 MIDI Time Piece interface.

Next you'll need a controller—a synthesizer or sound generator with a keyboard. The controller should have a minimum of 61 keys, the optimum of course is 88. Some keyboards are built specifically to be MIDI controllers. These might feature weighted piano-style keys and on-board keyboard mapping functions. Usually these controllers have limited sound-generating capability.

The final link in the MIDI chain is the sound generator (see Figure 2.10). Sound generators may be integral to the workstation, the controller keyboard, even the computer itself, or they may be additional rack-mount devices without keyboards. There are myriad sound generators on the market, and purchasing the right ones is largely a matter of taste (although there are some industry favorites). Sound generators can be analog or digital. Pay particular attention to the number of voices the machine has. This is a measure of the number of different notes the device can output at any given instant. Each of the voices can be assigned to the same sound or timbre, or they can be assigned to all different sounds in any combination. For example, if you have a 16-voice sound generator, you may assign 4 voices to the drum sound, 2 to the bass sound, 6 to the piano sound and 4 to the brass sound. At any given instant in this configuration, the sound generator can output a 6-note piano chord, 4 simultaneous drum hits, a 4-note brass harmony and a 2-note bass chord—quite a racket! A single 16- or 32-voice sound generator can output enough sounds to emulate an entire four-piece band.

Figure 2.10 Roland U-220 Sound Module.

Many sound generators also have built-in effects such as reverb, chorus, delay, compression, and expansion. This is useful for freeing up your outboard effects machines for vocals and other analog tracks. One last measure of the sound generator's flexibility is its number of outputs. It is often convenient to route different sounds to separate channels on the mixer. Some sound generators have only one stereo output for all voices, some have several, and others have a separate mono output for each voice, plus a mix or stereo mix output to which all voices are sent if you choose not to use the mono outputs.

An interesting note: When I set up my studio, I had two different rack-mount sound generators for the MIDI suite. Each had 8 mono outputs plus 2 stereo mix outputs on the back of the machines, so I set up my patchbay to receive 10 inputs from each machine. I then inserted plugs in each of the outputs and mounted the sound generators in their racks. As it turned out, I could not get any sound from the stereo mix outputs of either machine. After much fretting and poring over manuals, I realized that both machines were configured so that inserting plugs into each mono output jack defeated the stereo mix outputs. This was an undesirable situation, because on both machines, routing sounds to the individual outputs required some time-consuming programming every time I wanted to use a new sound configuration. This is OK for special situations, but not for every session. Also, the digital effects built into one of the units were not available at the mono outputs! None of this information was offered by the salespeople or by the user's manuals for these machines. It wasn't until I called the manufacturers that I verified it. I ended up having to reconfigure my patchbay and remove the mono output jacks during normal operation.

Samplers

Although often considered a part of the MIDI setup (many of the workstations and sound generators discussed above are capable of sampling), I prefer to discuss samplers under a separate section because of the usefulness of these machines. Unless you've been living in Siberia for the past few years, you are probably aware that a sampler is a device capable of taking an input sound and storing it to be played back or output on demand. Figure 2.11 shows a typical sampler.

Figure 2.11 The Akai S950 sampler.

The range of possibilities of these devices is incredible. Samplers have changed the face of the music industry in the nineties (in fact, rap and hip-hop music are based almost entirely on sampling). The sound quality of many professional samplers is superb—CD-quality or better. Sampling technology is used to re-create the natural sounds of acoustic instruments through electronic keyboards, resulting in full orchestral arrangements at the fingertips of virtually every composer. Sound effects, which at one time were added to movie soundtracks through a laborious process of live recording and tape editing, can now be inserted into a film sequence in minutes by using a sampler to re-create the sound at exactly the right moment.

With a sampler, you can digitally record short vocal or guitar tracks, and then play them back during mixdown at the times they should appear in the song. This alleviates the need to put those parts onto the analog tape machine, freeing up tracks and avoiding the sound degradation associated with analog tape. You can sample a cymbal, guitar, voice, or any other sound you like and program the sampler to replay the sound backwards. The only other way to get this effect is to record the sound on tape, and then replay it backwards—a time-consuming task. You can use the sampler to sample and store the sounds of drum kits that people bring into your studio, giving you access to those drum sounds for your own recordings (be sure to clear this with the drummer; there have been lawsuits initiated over who owns that sound). You can also sample the sounds of other synthesizers and store them for later use.

I hope I've convinced you that the sampler is a handy little device. Here are some of the specs you should pay attention to when purchasing one.

Number of Bits   The bit rate of a sampler tells how much information is transmitted by each internal command of the sampler's microprocessor. Bit rates range from 8 to over 20. 8- and 12-bit samplers are lower quality machines and should be avoided unless your budget is really tight. 16 bits is typical for most studio-quality machines. 18 and 20 bits are big-time, and so are the prices.

Sampling Rate   Refers to the number of times per second the sound waveform is sampled. The faster the sampling rate, the better the frequency response of the sampled sound. Most samplers have a user-definable range of sampling rates from 16 KHz to 48 Khz and higher. For sampling speaking voices and low-frequency sounds, the lower sampling rates can be used. For high-frequency stuff (like cymbals), you need to get into the 32-KHz and higher ranges to maintain fidelity. As you switch from low sample rates to high sample rates, you lose sampling time.

Sampling Time   The maximum length of the sampled sound. A good machine can sample at 48 KHz for 20–30 seconds or more. This gives you enough time to sample a chorus vocal, guitar solo, or even a 30-second commercial voice-over.

Disk Storage   Once you've sampled a sound, you need to store it. Most samplers store sounds to floppy disk, each of which can hold a few sounds, depending on the complexity of the sample. However, some samplers have built-in hard drives which allow for quick storage and retrieval of a large number of sounds. Several samplers have SCSI interfaces (pronounced "scuzzy"—isn't that nice?). This stands for Small Computer System Interface, and it allows you to connect an external hard drive to the machine for storing samples.

Some samplers are mono, others can sample in stereo. The cost for stereo is—you guessed it—about twice that for mono. Some other factors you may wish to consider when purchasing a sampler are the ease of operation, the type of sound manipulation available, and the extent of the library of sounds available for the product either through the manufacturer or in the public domain.

Synchronizers

A synchronizer reads time code from a master device (which may be an analog tape deck, a VCR, or a sequencer), and then outputs time code to the other devices in the chain. Since there are different types of time code, the synchronizer can read whatever type the master is using, then translate it into whatever type of code the slaves use. You can also use the synchronizer to trigger other machines at specific times, to program lag times, generate new time code or refresh old time code, or perform a host of other tricks useful to the operation of multiple machines.

Synchronization is a complex subject. I suggest reading a book on synchronization such as the one listed in Appendix A before attempting to lock all of your machines during a client session. However, for purchasing specs, your synchronizer should read and generate both SMPTE (pronounced "simptee" by almost everyone) and MIDI time codes. The Midiizer by Tascam (see Figure 2.12) or the Sync-Controller by Peavey will get the job done. A synchronizer used widely in professional studios is the Zeta III by Adams-Smith. Some high-end MIDI interfaces, like the MIDI Time Piece by Mark of the Unicorn or the Studio 3 and Studio 5 interfaces by Opcode, also perform synchronization as an added function. If you expect to be doing video projects, it would help to have a synchronizer that can read and generate Vertical Interval Time Code or VITC (pronounced "vitsee" by the real hot dogs). Mark of the Unicorn manufactures a reasonably priced VITC generator/reader called the Video Timepiece, worth checking out.

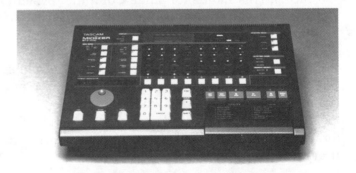

Figure 2.12   The Tascam Midiizer.

The Mixing Console

This is the brains of the whole operation. You're likely to spend a good chunk of your equipment budget on it. Mixers come in all shapes and sizes, they're made by a million different manufacturers, they're available new and used, and they all do pretty much the same thing. Throughout this book, I use the terms mixer, console and board interchangeably.

If at all possible, avoid using any mixer that was designed for sound reinforcement (live music or theater sound) in a recording studio. Although rugged and built to last, these consoles are generally not intended to meet the demands of a recording studio in terms of sound quality. Also, the architecture of the console (sends, returns, buses, and so on) is not likely to be suited to a recording studio situation.

Recording consoles come in two types, split consoles and in-line consoles. Split consoles have two different groups of channels: input channels and monitor channels. The groups are usually separated by the master control section of the board. The monitor channels are used to listen to the recorded tape tracks, and are usually less well equipped with EQ or auxiliary sends than the input channels.

In-line consoles have a single group of channels that function as both input channels and monitor channels. Neither design is better; each has advantages and disadvantages, and the choice is largely a matter of preference. I prefer split consoles; however, I know some accomplished audio engineers who would much rather work with in-line mixers. Figure 2.13 shows the Scorpion II, a moderately priced board manufactured by TAC, popular in many project studios.

Figure 2.13   The TAC Scorpion II console.

Before purchasing a recording console there are a number of design and performance factors that should be considered. I tried to list them in order of importance and found that I couldn't. Each aspect is important and should not be overlooked. The trick is to strike the right balance.

Sound Quality   Listen to the thing. Is it clear and noise free as you preview music coming through its main channel inputs? Does it tend to color the music (all of them do) in a good way? The most unfortunate aspect of purchasing a mixer is that it is not always possible to listen to it before you buy it. Even if you do, you'll probably be listening to each different mixer through different speakers and amplification systems. One idea is to bring a pair of headphones with you to each dealer, and perhaps your own program material (a CD or something).

Number of Channels   The number of input channels should be suitable for the type of music you intend to record. If you'll be using a 16-track tape machine plus a MIDI rig with 10 sound-generator outputs, you might have a total of 26 (or more) inputs active at any time. I would recommend at minimum a 32-input mixer in that situation. On most consoles, the channels (otherwise used as tape monitors and auxilliaries) can be used as additional inputs during mixdown, giving you much added input capability. For example, a 32 input mixer with 16 monitor channels and 6 auxilliary channels can send 54 channels at mixdown (32 + 16 + 6).

Input Types   You'll be expected to derive signals from a number of different types of sources such as microphones, guitars, keyboards, phonograph outputs (for sampling) or anything else you can think of. The mixer channel inputs should be flexible—they should allow you to connect either 1/4-inch plugs or XLR cables and should have switchable Mike/Line level controls. An added plus is 48-volt power. Certain types of microphones require power to operate, and many consoles supply this power through their microphone inputs. This is called phantom power.

Auxiliary and Effects Sends   Modern production techniques require a considerable amount of effects processing on almost every instrument. The effects send buses and auxiliary send buses are circuit paths that allow you to add an adjustable amount of effect such as reverb or delay from an outboard effects device to each input channel. You can also use auxiliary sends as headphone mix channels for the musicians in the studio, or for a separate monitor mix. For recording purposes, a console should have at least two effects sends per channel, preferably four to eight effects and/or auxiliary sends.

Subgroups   These are most commonly used as tape sends. You can route any of your mixer input channels to one or more subgroups, and each subgroup can then be assigned to an input on the multitrack. Although not necessary, it helps to have as many subgroups as there are tape tracks; that is, for sixteen track recording, the optimum mixing console would have 16 subgroups. It is also possible during mixdown to assign groups of instruments to a subgroup, allowing control of an entire drum set, for example, from a single fader. When looking at console specs, you'll see either two, three, or four numbers, separated by *x* or *by*. The first number is the number of input channels. The second number is usually the number of subgroups, the third number represents the master sends and sometimes a fourth number is included to indicate the number of monitor channels. Thus, a 32x8x2x16 board has 32 inputs, 8 subgroups, a stereo master, and 16 monitor channels.

Dimensions   How much space do you have in your control room? Don't let your eyes get bigger than your head–some consoles take up a lot of room, and you don't want engineers, producers and musicians to be climbing all over each other and your equipment just because you went for the mondo mixer. If you have the room and the money, a large, impressive-looking console will sometimes attract more clients than a small, even sonically superior mixer. You decide. However, if you're in a really tight space, or if you need portability, you might consider a rack-mount mixer (see Figure 2.14), of which there are many new quality models on the market.

EQ Section   Now you're talking about performance. One of the things you'll ask of your console is the ability to take a perfectly horrible input signal and make it sound good. Of course the general rule of recording is "garbage in, garbage out," but in some cases, with the right amount of equalization, a drab vocal can be made to shine or a thin drum can become full and punchy. The EQ section on some consoles (such as the Neve, SSL and Focusrite boards) is so good that studios will pay hundreds of thousands of dollars to own them. A better choice (even if you have that kind of money) might be to buy a less expensive mixer and use a separate, high quality equalizer or preamplifier at the input. You can even purchase one or more Neve or SSL input modules (still not cheap) and use them as input preamplifiers for your moderately priced board.

Figure 2.14   Tascam rack-mount mixers.

Noise Floor and Crosstalk   Disconnect all inputs to your console. Turn up all the faders and the control room volume to the maximum. The hiss that you hear from your control-room speakers is the noise floor of your console—the amount of noise that the console itself contributes to the audio signal path. Although you can't expect a board priced below $20,000 to be amazingly quiet, it shouldn't sound like Niagara Falls. Crosstalk is a measure of the amount of signal that bleeds from the channel where it belongs to a channel where it doesn't belong. Most boards exhibit some degree of crosstalk; however, it should be minimal.

Automation   Mixer automation has become available for most mixing boards and is an incredibly useful feature. It tends to be expensive (in the case of lower-priced boards, automation may be more than the board itself), but keep in mind that it does not have to be purchased with the board—you can add it at a later date. Automation allows some or all of the mixer's functions to be controlled by a computer linked to time code. As you mix, the computer is remembering all the fader movements and muting actions that you perform (some also remember EQ settings, AUX sends, Pannings, etc.). These can be played back, recreating the mix in real time over and over again. If the mix needs small adjustments, you can make them as you play back, allowing you to tweak the mix until you've got it perfect. If you've ever manually mixed a 24- or 32-input program, you know what a fantastic feature this is.

There are two types of automation, moving fader and VCA (voltage controlled amplifier) automation. With VCA, the fader values are controlled, but the faders themselves do not physically move. In moving fader automation, the faders move by themselves via small servo-motors controlled by the computer. Not only does this look pretty funky (you can watch the ghostly movements for hours—it's like staring into a fish tank), but it is handy, since you don't have to reset all the faders to their correct positions before making a change to the mix, as you might have to do for some types of VCA automation. Moving fader automation is sonically better than VCA, as the signal does not pass through an additional amplifier section.

Price   Mixing consoles range in price from hundreds of dollars for a small rack-mount mixer to about three-quarters of a million dollars for a 72-input Focusrite console. A $2500 console and a $250,000 console may have the same number of inputs, outputs, and buses, so what makes for the price disparity? Sound quality is the main thing. As mentioned before, all consoles tend to color the sound somewhat, but board manufacturers like Neve and SSL have developed reputations for incredible sounding electronics and, as such, these boards draw high-paying clients. In the way of features, the expensive boards may have some added bells and whistles, such as compression and noise gating on each input, and they are designed to stand up to constant usage; however, the basic working layout of both high-end and low-end boards is the same. It is certainly possible to create an excellent recording with a $2500 console.

Outboard Effects

If you are familiar with multitrack recording, then you probably have a good understanding of the functions of most effects in the signal processing world. The following is a list of those processors that I consider to be essential to the well-equipped studio:

- Reverb
- Delay
- Chorus
- Flange
- Compressor/Limiter
- Noise Gate
- Graphic or parametric equalizer
- Aural Exciter Sonic Maximizer

It is now possible to purchase a single Digital Signal Processor (DSP) that will perform all of the above functions and more. However, chances are that you will want to use one or more of these functions on different signals at different times, so having just one machine will probably not cut it.

As a bare-bones minimum, I would recommend purchasing a single processor for all of the first four functions (such as an Alesis Quadraverb, shown in Figure 2.15, Yamaha SPX 1000, or Lexicon LXP Series), and then obtaining separate units for Compression, Noise Gate, EQ and Exciter. Although it is often economical to buy multifunction processors such as these, as a general rule dedicated single-function processors exhibit better sound quality.

Figure 2.15 Alesis Quadraverb.

Compressors, expanders and gates are known as dynamics processors, because they all modify the signal level in some way. Compression is one of the most useful signal processing tricks. It allows you to keep signal levels relatively constant in tough situations, such as when the lead vocalist prances about the microphone, one moment pinning the meters, the next moment barely whispering. It also brings a final stereo mix to life, accentuating drum hits and bringing "lost" instruments back into the game. A good compressor can add a lot to the quality of recordings made under poor conditions.

Noise gates are essential for keeping guitar amps quiet until it's their turn to speak, for gated reverb effects, and for keeping vocal tracks free of coughs and scuffling feet. Some noise gates also double as expanders (the opposite of compressors), which are great for keeping adjacent drums from bleeding into each other's microphones, or adding dynamics to a flat-sounding mix.

A separate equalizer allows you more control over the harmonic and tonal content of a recorded sound. There may be instances where you'll want to adjust the tonality of an entire stereo mix, and this cannot be done acceptably using the console channel EQ. Also, a discrete equalizer can sometimes be used to key in on and eliminate noise in a certain frequency band. Coupled to the sidechain input of a compressor, the equalizer can be used to control the compressor's output for things like de-essing a vocal track.

Finally, the Aural Exciter, which is a trademark of Aphex Systems (similar devices are made by BBE, Inc. under the moniker of "Sonic Maximizers"), are "psychoacoustic processors," which means that nobody really knows what they do, except that they really make stuff sound nice. Use this baby—with discretion—on vocals, guitars, keyboards and full mixes and listen to the sound-quality enhancement!

Figure 2.16   The Aphex Aural Exciter.

Mixdown Decks

People mix down to everything nowadays. If you're on a tight budget, you mix down to a good cassette deck. It helps to get one with three heads so that you can monitor off the tape, meaning you can hear the final product as it's recording. (Two-head tape decks let you listen only to the input signal, so that if the taped signal is messed up, you may only hear it later as you listen back.) Another possibility is to mix down to a hi-fi VCR, some of which have superior sound-recording capability.

Until recently, the really cool thing to mix down to was 1/2-inch analog 30IPS Dolby SR 2-track. Quality 1/2-inch mixdown machines are very expensive (over $5000 if you're interested), as is the tape that goes in them (about $40 for 16 minutes of tape), but the sound quality is superb. Recently, however, the trend is shifting to DAT or digital audio tape (see Figure 2.17) for mixdown, and this is good news. First of all, the sonic performance of a DAT deck is as good or better than a CD player. Second, compared to high-end analog 2-track machines, DATs are cheap, ranging in price from $650 to $2500 for quality machines. In my opinion, the DAT is the machine of choice. Some of the models are portable, and can be used to mix or record remote sources. Since it does not degrade the signal at all (stop screaming, purists), you can use DAT to transfer tracks from one medium to another, for example, from someone's home MIDI setup to the studio multitrack. It can also be used to archive information from various digital workstations. Some of the newer professional DAT machines can be synced to time code, adding greatly to their already impressive versatility.

Figure 2.17   The Tascam DA-30 DAT.

Digital Audio Workstations

In the audio industry, it is often not enough to live in the present; you must ride the wave of the future at all times to stay in business. If you subscribe to that philosophy, perhaps you should consider a Digital Audio Workstation, even if it's the only piece of equipment you buy.

DAWs are essentially multiple-channel sampling machines with long sampling times; the number of channels or tracks available usually ranges from 2 to 48. (Figures 2.18 and 2.19 show two recently developed digital audio workstations.) There are two types of DAWs: hard disk recorders and tape-based digital recorders.

Figure 2.18   The Korg Sound Link DAW.

Figure 2.19   The Roland DM-80 DAW.

On a hard disk recorder, digital tracks do not have to be recorded in a linear sequence. You can record different song parts in various empty places along the track—this frees up a lot of track space and gives an 8-track hard disk recorder about as much recording capability as an analog 12-track machine. You give each section of track a name or address code and create a playlist indicating when each address code should be read by the machine. As the song is played back, the computer accesses parts of the track in the order you specify.

This cannot be done on tape-based DAWs (see Figure 2.20), since the digital tape is read in real time, as on an analog machine. The advantage to tape-based DAWs is storage. The digital tape that is used to record the material is also used as the archive master. The hard disk information must be downloaded either to another hard disk or to some tape format (such as DAT) for storage.

Figure 2.20   Alesis ADAT Digital 8-track Recorder.

Just about every DAW on the market today functions as its own mixer, with all parameters under computer control—a self-contained, automated mixdown facility. In addition, many of them have internal MIDI sequencers and/or allow manipulation of MIDI data, and nearly all are able to lock to both internal and external SMPTE time code. Some DAWs even have built-in Digital Signal Processing. Prices for DAWs range between $2500 per track for the less expensive machines to over $20,000 per track for high-end devices such as the New England Digital Synclavier system.

There is one drawback. At the present time there is no interface standard for DAWs. In English, that means if you record something on your DAW, chances are you won't be able to play it back, modify it or otherwise transfer the data to any other manufacturer's DAW. Eventually there will be a standard protocol for DAW data. I hope it comes soon.

The Monitoring Section

Another happy development in studio technology is a recent shift in preferences on the part of most modern-day recording engineers to near-field monitoring. Traditionally studios installed large, wildly expensive speaker systems relatively far away (more than a few feet) from the engineer's listening point. These were driven, sometimes at frightful SPLs, by banks of wildly expensive high-wattage amplifiers. To accommodate the exaggerated acoustic effects, wildly expensive architectural acoustic treatments were incorporated into the control room design.

Luckily, someone figured out that if you use a pair of small but highly accurate monitor speakers, powered by a small but very clean amplifier, and place them relatively near the listening area (less than a few feet, usually right on top of the console bridge), you will actually achieve better results than you will with the nuclear-powered system described above. This is known as *near-field* monitoring. The main benefit of near-field monitoring is that the close proximity of the sound source reduces the effect of room acoustics on the engineer's perception of the program sound. The other, obvious benefit is that you spend less on speakers, you spend less on amplification and you spend less on acoustic treatment.

Figure 2.21　Peavey PRM 3105 Monitors.

There is a difference between *speakers* and *monitors*. Don't make the mistake of purchasing those stereo speakers you've been lusting after for your living room and installing them in your studio. Consumer stereo speakers are designed to sound pleasing to the average listener. This means they might roll off a little on the high frequencies, or add a little boost to the bass. This may sound nice, but "nice" is not what you want in a studio. You want accuracy. Studio monitors are designed to come as close as possible to a flat response (the word *flat* refers to the graph of speaker output over a certain frequency range), that is, what you've got is what you hear.

Good near-field monitors can be purchased for as little as $180 per pair. Top-of-the-line near-fields, such as the Meyer HD-1, cost as much as $4000 per pair. Some good but considerably less expensive monitors are the Yamaha NS-10M (see Figure 2.22) and the Tannoy PBM 6.5.

Figure 2.22 Yamaha NS-10M Monitors.

Monitoring and mixing with headphones is possible but not advisable. There are some critical differences between listening to monitors as opposed to listening with headphones. First, the stereo image is somewhat unrealistic through headphones. The stereo spread is wider with monitors. You actually feel sound through your body, a sensation which is lost with headphones. Finally, the frequency response of headphones varies as you press them closer to you head or pull them further apart. If you must monitor with headphones, AKG makes a line of headphones specifically designed for monitoring and mixing (see Figure 2.23). They exhibit pretty good spatial quality (for headphones, that is).

As far as amplification is concerned, you need to know how loud you intend to monitor and how efficient your monitor speakers are. Efficiency is a measure of how much power it takes to drive speakers at a given SPL. Some speakers can crank at 105db with 30 watts of power, others need 50 watts before you can even hear them. Let's say you prefer to monitor at about 85db. If your monitors require 70 watts per channel to sustain 85db, you should consider an amplifier that is rated at least 120 watts per channel. This will allow the amplifier to faithfully reproduce transients above 85db without distorting (if the amplifier is providing maximum power at your normal listening levels, funny things start to happen as peaks in the music go beyond the amp's capability to reproduce them). It will also allow you to goose the level past 85db every once in a while without maxing out your amp.

Figure 2.23   AKG K240 Monitor Headphones.

Finally, the output impedance of the amplifier must be matched to the input impedance of your monitors. The lower the impedance of an output, the more current it can deliver, and the lower the impedance of an input, the more current it requires. The optimum situation occurs when the input impedance of a speaker and the output impedance of the amplifier are equal. Amplifier/monitor matching is so critical to the sound of the system that many of the newer monitors (such as the Meyers mentioned above) are designed with matched amplifiers built in. Figure 2.24 shows a typical stereo amplifier.

Figure 2.24   Peavey PMA 200 Amplifier.

Microphones

Good microphones are an absolute necessity in any studio. There are three common types of microphones in use: dynamic, ribbon and condenser types. I won't go into the inner workings of each; suffice it to say that the different types of microphone have different sound characteristics associated with them. Experience will give you a feel for what type of microphone to use in each situation. Dynamic mikes tend to sound "warm" while condensers are very "crisp" sounding. Most condenser microphones require phantom 48-volt power to be supplied by the console or by a separate power supply. Ribbon microphones, which have a very warm and pleasant sound, are an older design, and are not as popular today as they were 30 or 40 years ago because they tend to be fragile. Most modern dynamic and condenser mikes can handle incredibly loud sounds; however, a well-placed cough can ruin a ribbon microphone.

A good idea may be to purchase one "Cadillac" microphone to perform the delicate stuff, like vocals and acoustic guitars, and some less expensive workhorses to mike amplifiers and drums. At the moderate-to-high end, there are two very popular microphone standards in the recording industry: the AKG 414 (shown in Figure 2.25) and the Neumann U87. Both are rather expensive but well worth the price. The Neumann lists for about $2500 and the AKG lists for $1399. Although the Neumann is nearly twice the price, it is not necessarily twice as good as the AKG. Many artists prefer the AKG when given a choice, and it is largely a matter of taste. If you have never worked with one of these mikes before, you might be amazed at the quality they can impart to the sound of your tracks.

Figure 2.25 The AKG 414 microphone.

If you can't squeeze one of those into your budget, I recommend purchasing at least one medium-grade microphone such as an EV 357, the AKG 451, or the Sennheiser 441 or 421 (shown in Figure 2.26), which will set you back about three to four hundred dollars. Still too much? A Shure SM58 is a good all-purpose microphone that can be purchased for roughly $100.

Figure 2.26   The Sennheiser 421 microphone.

If you'll be recording drums, guitar amps, bass amps and similar instruments, a few Shure SM57s (see Figure 2.27) are a must. These little workhorses sound really good and cost less than $100 apiece. Another recommendation is the AKG D112, which looks like a big egg. This mike is designed for low-frequency applications such as kick drums and bass amplifiers. It is not very expensive (about $250) and will find plenty of use in your microphone collection.

Figure 2.27   Shure SM57.

Test and Maintenance Equipment

The more complex your rig becomes, the more you'll have to deal with testing, maintaining, troubleshooting and fixing the equipment. A few well-placed dollars on test and maintenance equipment can save you hundreds in outside-shop repair costs, even if you know little about electronic equipment repair. For example, being able to locate a faulty wire leading into a device might save you from being raked over the coals by some repair shop that opens the unit, finds nothing wrong, and charges you $100 for the effort.

Analog tape machines require head demagnetization, which means you'll have to buy a demagnetizer. Don't forget to pick up tape head-cleaning fluid and rubber cleaner for the rubber rollers in the tape path of the multitracks.

In most recording studios, fixed-frequency oscillators are used to calibrate tape speeds. Some mixing consoles have built-in oscillators, and can output several set frequencies, such as 100Hz, 1KHz, and 10KHz. These are printed onto the tape before the recording session. At a later session, or in another studio, engineers can use these identified signals to adjust the speed of the tape machine to match the original recording conditions.

A digital multimeter or DMM is a very useful device for measuring voltage, current, and resistance of electric circuits, and many have built-in continuity-checking features which help locate breaks in wires or faulty ground circuits.

As you get more familiar with the workings of electronic audio equipment, you should consider purchasing an oscilloscope. A oscilloscope will allow you to measure voltage, phase delay, noise and many other things. It is indispensable for tape head alignment. The important feature is that you can actually see the waveform under investigation. Before purchasing a oscilloscope, be sure to determine your particular needs, because it is possible to get into some serious overkill. The speed of the oscilloscope, in Hertz, will play a large part in determining its price. For measuring frequencies within the range of human hearing (20Hz to 20KHz), you would need a bandwidth of roughly 40KHz (twice the highest observable frequency). You don't want to get into expensive Megahertz-rated oscilloscopes or digital-storage oscilloscope technology unless you'll be measuring digital clock pulses or stuff like that.

If you really want to get serious, there are special test machines designed to measure Total Harmonic Distortion (THD), spectrum analyzers for observing harmonics, even computer-based analyzers for measuring the acoustic responses of a room. However, most of these machines require a knowledgeable operator. In the rare event that you find a pressing need for one of these highly specialized devices, they are available for rent through a number of test equipment dealers.

Summary

The equipment list is, in some respects, an agonizing one to generate. It involves considerable compromise and is always subject to personal tastes. Chances are your decisions about equipment will change as time goes by and you become aware of new developments in the industry. Since product development is currently going on at a breakneck pace, there is sometimes a tendency to put off equipment decisions for fear of becoming obsolete overnight. While this type of paranoia may have some validity in the business world, it does not hold much water if your main concern is creativity. No matter what kind of device comes out tomorrow, it will not effect your ability to create great works with what you have today.

Trust your instincts, but don't be swayed by a slick advertising campaign or a sly salesperson. If you're not sure about any aspect of a given piece of equipment, suspend making a decision until you get more information. If a manufacturer or company representative is evasive or otherwise seems to be holding back information, be concerned—there is usually a good reason for it. Know exactly what you need to accomplish with each piece and in making your list, prioritize each item, listing those that you can do without if necessary and those that are essential.

Don't forget to leave yourself open to expand. Try not to purchase equipment that will be working at its maximum capacity in your present configuration. Leave room in your layout for interconnection of equipment that will be added at a later date.

When specifying the equipment for the studio, try to imagine the entire facility as a single device, built for the purpose of making recordings. The device will be constructed of many smaller individual parts designed to work together toward a single purpose. Thinking along these lines will keep you tuned into the necessity for compatibility, steer you away from redundancy, and keep you focused on what you really need.

BUDGETING: ALL THOSE THINGS YOU DIDN'T THINK ABOUT

Budgeting is the assessment of funds available, and the judicial allocation of those funds to cover each aspect of the project. How much should be spent on construction, and how much does that leave for equipment purchases? Which equipment should be purchased, and how much will it cost to own and operate it over the years?

Business owners may also want to consider doing some forecasting, including research and market study to determine the rate of return on a purchased piece of equipment, new service offered, or some other investment of time or money. If this $100,000 machine is purchased, will it generate $100,000 worth of business? Even if it does, it is possible that the purchase of an alternative $20,000 machine will bring $60,000 worth of business? Which situation is more desirable? I'll leave the mechanics of forecasting to the marketing and finance textbooks.

Realistic budgeting is a notoriously difficult thing to do. Even multi-million-dollar companies don't get it right most of the time, and the government almost never seems to be successful. Luckily, you won't have to deal with politics or big business, so you've got a chance at coming up with an accurate budget. The trick is to divorce your emotional desires from your calculations. When you get to the last few dollars, and you've just seen an ad for a new sound generator that can emulate Mick Jagger's voice via MIDI, it's tempting to shave a few bucks off the patchbay allocation to satisfy the overwhelming urge to own a Jagger-in-a-box. Of course if you do that, you'll invariably find yourself having to dump more money into your inferior patchbay and—bingo!—you're over budget.

These are some of the mistakes people nearly always make when budgeting:

1. They are overly optimistic about available funds.

2. They are unrealistic about the actual cost of the required items.

3. They don't take into account the increase in price that may occur between budgeting time and purchasing time.

4. They don't count the small stuff.

Item 4 is by far the most common and quite possibly the most expensive mistake. It is too easy to spend every last cent to get the machine with the extra bells and whistles, forgetting (or not wanting to remember) that you need to buy 25 connector cables at $25 each to connect it to your system.

Budget Considerations

Let's examine some of the most commonly overlooked items in home studio budgets.

Audio Wire and Cable

As pointed out in Chapter 2, a 16-track studio can require as much as 2 miles of wire for audio connections, depending on the specific design. At Bon Marché Productions (Studio B in the examples), I have an equipment cabinet with five Digital Signal Processors, three mixdown decks and a CD player. Each of these nine devices has a left and right input (except the CD player) and a left and right output. That's a total of 34 inputs and outputs. These are each routed to the patchbay, which requires roughly 15 feet of wire. That's 34 × 15 feet, or 510 feet of wire just to wire up one small equipment cabinet, and that only gets you to the patchbay. From the patchbay, most of those signals are routed to the mixing console and back again to the bay, probably using another 500 or 600 feet of wire. Therefore, to operate those nine machines, I use 1,100 feet of signal wire! A good price for 3-conductor shielded hook-up wire is about $.08 per foot, or roughly $88.00 for one little cabinet of equipment.

At the end of each wire is a connector, either a quarter-inch mono, quarter-inch stereo, or XLR-type connector. The average cost of quarter-inch connectors is $2 each, $3 each for XLR. This results in a connector cost of roughly $70 at the cabinet and $70 at the console. At this point, the total cost to make all the connections for this cabinet comes in at about $228.

Of the nine machines just discussed, three are MIDI-controllable. To take advantage of this, at least one MIDI cable must be run from the MIDI "in" jack of each machine to the interface or the MIDI patchbay—a distance of about 10 feet. A ten-foot MIDI cable with 5-pin connectors on each end costs about $12. Add $36 to the last figure to bring the connection cost to $264. If you want to do system-exclusive dumps from those machines into your computer (a method for saving configuration information), you need to add another cable per machine. Add another $36. The total connection cost for the cabinet is now a nice, neat $300.

Figure 3.1 shows the complete MIDI connection diagram for the studio. Add up all the cables and consider an average length of 10 feet per cable (which is optimistic); the total figure is 22 MIDI cables for this system. Do the math yourself.

All this is for only one equipment cabinet. From the patchbay, there are 25 audio connections to the studio input stations. There are about 150 connections to the console. There are 36 connections to the MIDI rack. Finally, there are 36 connections to the analog open-reel decks. I don't mean to scare you out of studio design and into the dry-cleaning business; I simply want to impress upon you the necessity of budgeting a sufficient amount to accomplish the necessary wiring. It's easier and cheaper to do this much wiring if you buy all the materials in one bulk purchase, rather than pick up a few connectors one week, and a few more the next.

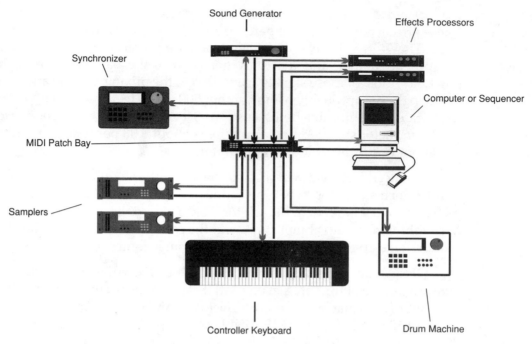

Figure 3.1 MIDI connections for the studio.

Racks and Stands

In a studio, a microphone is useless without a stand. The old emergency method of taping it to a chair or some other inanimate object gets tiresome fast. Whenever you budget for a microphone, budget for a stand along with it. You'll thank yourself. Also, many applications require the use of a boom stand, which incorporates a horizontal arm mounted to the vertical stand. You can't mike an guitar amplifier, for example, with a straight stand unless you raise the amp up off the floor until the speakers are waist level. If you're trying to lift a Marshall stack, you'll wish you had a boom instead. Drums require precision mike placement, which you really can't accomplish without a boom stand.

You'll also need rack stands for your rack-mount equipment and perhaps special stands or furniture for the multitrack and the console. These are rarely, if ever included in the price of the machine, and the cost may surprise you.

Furnishings

Like it or not, your studio will require places to sit, places to write, and places to store things.

It's hard to look at the last few hundred dollars in your budget and say, "We've got enough money for another AKG 414, but we really need a couple of chairs and a file cabinet." Still, if you're going to be parked in front of the console for 16 hours a day, you'll find yourself wishing you could trade that AKG in for a comfortable replacement to the milk crate you're sitting on. Clients appreciate comfort also, and sometimes a few hundred dollars on a couch for the control room is well spent.

Outside Services

No matter how handy you are, there are always a few things you can't do yourself. You've got to pay the phone company to install telephone service if you need it. If you require an electrical service upgrade, you'll have to hire a licensed electrician. In fact, any electrical wiring that is part of the construction should be done by a licensed electrician as well.

Unless you own a truck or a dumpster, you'll need someone to haul your construction debris to a dump site. You may want to hire some technical assistance, such as a consultant to help you design your acoustical space or connect and troubleshoot your system. Sometimes your local audio dealers will offer such services.

Equipment Service Contracts

If you can't afford downtime, or if you aren't equipped to perform your own maintenance and repair, you may want to look into service contracts on the equipment. These will add to the price of the machine, but may be well worth it over time.

Sales Tax

Depending on where you live, sales tax could add a healthy amount to your final bill. Be careful.

Putting Together a Rough Estimate Budget

In the first example, Studio A (a single-room, small-multitrack/MIDI setup), little or no construction is involved. The money required to put the studio together is a little over $10,000, with no financing anticipated.

Studio B is a real-life example, and the table shown is the proposed budget for my studio, Bon Marché Productions. The studio is more involved, and is intended to operate as a business. As described earlier, it consists of a control room, and a sound lock with two doors leading to a talent room with an integral isolation booth. All audio connections lead to a patchbay, and the talent room includes 6 input stations, each with its own headphone input, Mike input and Line level input. The control room houses a 16-track analog tape deck, a 32x8x2x16 console, outboard effects and a full MIDI setup with a computer sequencer.

Once you've gone through the design phases described in Chapters 2 and 3, you'll have a good idea of what the studio will do, the type of equipment you need, and how you plan to use the space. It is helpful to put this information into the form of an estimate as shown in Tables 3.1 and 3.2.

Appendix C contains a sample worksheet that can be used for equipment budget estimations.

Table 3.1 Proposed budget for Studio A.

Item	Cost
8-track open-reel deck	$ 3000
16x8x2 mixing board, rack-mount	2500
MIDI workstation	1600
Synchronizer	750
Digital Signal Processor (reverb, delay, chorus)	425
Mixdown deck, cassette	350
Compressor/Limiter/Gate	350
Power amp	300
Monitors	300
Microphone	250
Connectors, cable, recording tape, incidentals	250
Total	**$10,075**

All of the values shown are revisable, and represent the initial apportioning process arrived at by shopping around and talking to dealers. There is some give and take here, plus some matters of personal preference. Someone else with the same budget and different taste would come up with a completely different plan.

What's important is to determine where you will splurge and where you will sacrifice. For example, it is possible to obtain a functional, rack-mount 16-input mixer for as little as $1800; however, a higher priced unit was preferred in this case because of the additional flexibility it offered. The same was true for the Digital Signal Processor. As a result, sacrifices were made in the microphone and power amp allocations. The amount of money allocated for cable and connectors was probably insufficient also, and additional cable may have to be purchased over time.

Table 3.2   Proposed budget for Studio B.

Equipment

Item	Cost
32x16x2 console	$10,000
16-track open-reel deck	5,500
Macintosh IIci computer	4,000
Patchbay, wiring, and connectors	2,100
MIDI controller and sound generator	2,000
Sampler	1,500
Mixdown deck (DAT)	1,300
MIDI interface and synchronizer	1,000
Digital Signal Processors (2)	900
Compressor/Limiter/Gate (2)	900
Vocal mike	850
Power amplifier	500
Monitors	500
Drum and instrument mikes (5)	450
Mixdown deck (cassette)	350
1/3-octave stereo equalizer	350
MIDI patchbay	300
Sequencing software	300
Aural exciter	200
Headphone amplifier	150
Microphone stands	120
Headphones (3)	100
Wiring stations (5)	100
Total equipment	**$33,470**

Construction

Item	Cost
Carpet and flooring	$1,200
Service panel upgrade	900
Lighting fixtures	300
Insulation	300
Doors and door hardware	300
Electrical wiring and outlets	200
Molding and finishing	200
Window glass	200
Sheetrock and wallboard	192
Lumber (studs)	180
Spackle and paint	150
Trash removal	150
Telephone-line installation	150
Fasteners (nails, screws, glue)	75
Acoustic caulking	25
Total construction	**$4,522**

Other items

Item	Cost
Acoustic treatment	$1,500
Alarm system	500
Cabinet	500
Air conditioners	500
Chairs	450
Power-line conditioners	300
Telephone and answering machine	150
Total other items	$3,900
Grand total	**$41,932**

Calculating Construction Costs

First, establish an overall construction design and take measurements to determine the amount of floor, wall, and ceiling space to be constructed. According to the diagram of Studio B (see Figure 3.2), there is a total of 52 feet of new framed wall. Walls A, B, C and D were already framed and do not require reconstruction. One of the walls is an isolating wall requiring double framing (see Chapter 4), so this dimension is added twice, resulting in a total of 65 feet of wall.

Standard construction practice requires that studs be located a maximum of 16 inches apart measured from center to center. Divide the number of feet of wall by 16 inches to get 48.75 as the number of vertical studs required. Since you will be purchasing 8-foot studs, take the total amount of wall space in feet, multiply by 2 (top and bottom) and divide by 8 to determine how many studs you will need for upper and lower frame headers. Add 20% for waste, double-framing windows, and so on. The final estimate is 80 studs.

At $2.25 per stud, the projected cost for lumber is $180.00.

Sheetrock comes in 4-foot by 8-foot, or 32-square-foot, panels. Calculate the total area in square feet of wall and ceiling space that needs to be covered, and then divide that by 32 to get the number of panels. In my case, I had to account for both sides of the isolating wall and the outer isolation-booth walls, and I decided to double the Sheetrock on the studio side of the isolating wall for acoustic reasons. With 8-foot ceilings, the total area is approximately 1570 square feet. Divide by 32 and add 10% for waste; the final figure is 55 panels. At 3.50 per panel, the projected cost is $192.00.

Insulation is usually sold by the linear foot. To estimate the amount of insulation required, you must consider that, for the eight-foot walls, each 16-inch space between frames will require an 8 foot length of insulation. Divide the wall length in inches by 16 and multiply by 8 to get an estimate of the number of linear feet of insulation needed for the walls. Do the same with each of the ceilings.

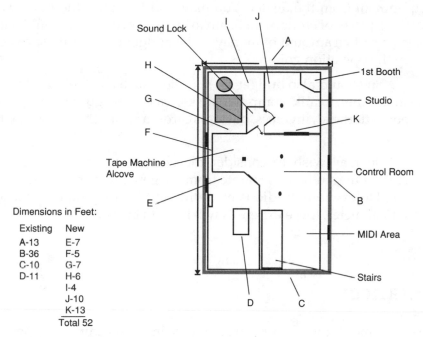

Figure 3.2 The layout for Studio B.

Dimensions in Feet:

Existing	New
A-13	E-7
B-36	F-5
C-10	G-7
D-11	H-6
	I-4
	J-10
	K-13
	Total 52

Related Expenses

There may be expenses related to owning and operating the studio that are separate from the fixed costs of equipment and construction. These include maintenance and repair costs, which will vary with time. Most equipment is under warranty the first 90 days of operation, and some equipment may be covered for as long as one to two years as part of the purchase price. It is often possible to purchase extensions on the warranties of new or used equipment from the dealer. You may find that after the first year or so, various pieces of equipment begin to break down, and it would help to set aside a certain amount of money in the budget to cover these expenses to keep the operation going.

You should also budget for supplies, such as blank mastering tape, head cleaner, blank computer disks, cassettes, guitar strings, printer paper, letterhead, invoices, business cards, and anything else you happen to use.

You may wish to consider the energy expenses associated with operating the studio as separate from the general energy expense of your home. Unless your studio is on a different heating zone and a separate electrical meter, these expenses will have to be estimated.

Insurance

Your home studio equipment should be insured against damage or theft. Most homeowner's policies will cover the equipment; however, you should consult your agent as to the amount of coverage you have. Most policies will give you only what they consider to be fair value for the equipment at the time of the loss; so if the mixing console you paid $10,000 for is stolen after three years, the insurance company will depreciate the unit and give you what they think is its present value. You may end up with only half of what you paid for the machine, or less. For a slight increase in premium, you can get what is known as "full replacement value," which means that upon loss, you'll be reimbursed the full price of a replacement machine.

You should provide your insurance company with a complete list of your equipment, including the retail value of each piece and, if possible, photographs of each unit. Do this even if they don't ask for it, and keep a copy of the whole package yourself to reduce the possibility of hassles in the event you put in a claim.

Most homeowner's policies will not cover equipment used for business purposes. As soon as you begin to operate as a business, you are no longer insured. In this case you need to purchase special musical equipment insurance. Some companies will offer this as a rider to your homeowner's policy. This type of insurance is also available through the

American Federation of Musicians (the musicians' union), although you must become a member to buy the insurance. Prices vary considerably, so shop around. My particular policy costs about $300 per year for $40,000 worth of equipment.

Dealing with Dealers

I understand that most studios are put together gradually, adding pieces over the years as money becomes available.

Obviously, not everyone with a home studio starts with a lump sum and no equipment, purchasing everything in one fell swoop. However, the closer you can get to making a single all-encompassing purchase, the more you'll get for your money. You'll be tempted to go out and buy as much equipment as you can with the money that you have, and continue in this manner, purchasing a little at a time. Technically, there is nothing wrong with this approach; however, it's amazing how much you can save by purchasing everything in one shot from a single dealer.

Once the dealer realizes that you intend to buy a package of equipment, and that you're shopping seriously among several dealers, he will do his best to get you the lowest possible price. Plus, if you're buying many pieces of equipment, the dealer can afford to discount much further than in the case of a single item. Most of the equipment for Studio B was purchased in a single stop from a single dealer. At one point, I had dealers offering to throw in monitor speakers, microphones, cases of tape and other items worth hundreds of dollars, just to complete the sale. In the end, my actual cost was 20% lower than the figures shown on the projected budget, which was put together using prices quoted by several dealers on individual pieces.

Some dealers may offer assistance in designing, connecting or trouble-shooting your equipment. It is possible that they will provide this service for free as customer support if you purchase a significant amount of merchandise. My local dealers were very helpful in answering questions as we got further and further into my design, and one of them even came down to the studio to explain some things about interconnection of devices. Remember, the dealers (at least the smart ones) want you to succeed, because it guarantees them a return customer.

Not everyone lives within a stone's throw of four or five professional audio dealers, so you don't have to buy locally. You can order from out of state, and most professional audio dealers will work with you over the phone. You just have to know what you want. A problem with making comparisons from one dealer's package to the next is that not all dealers handle the same equipment lines. Very often you'll hear "I don't sell those Zilswitch 402 compressors, but I'll give you a Zwickleham 251 compressor for the same price." You'd better do your homework and verify that this substitute is as good as the one you originally specced out. Don't take his word for it—as honest as he may be, he might not have a clue as to what your preferred device can do.

You'll also want to discuss service (or "dealer support"), and herein lies the disadvantage to buying from a nonlocal dealer. In many cases, the service contract or warranty requires that you return the equipment to the manufacturer, so there's no loss there. However in the case of dealers who offer their own service contracts, some will provide loaner units that you can use in place of your broken machine—resulting in zero downtime for the studio. If you're running a business, this can be very valuable.

Financing

You may consider borrowing money to build your dream studio. There are several different types of loans available from financial institutions and other sources.

Unsecured Personal Loans

These are the most expensive loans, bearing the highest interest rates since the bank has no real collateral in case you default. The bank simply checks out your income and credit rating and decides whether or not you can afford the loan. They don't ask you what you're going to use it for, but they might require you to keep a certain amount of cash on deposit with the bank. Using a personal loan to finance a large sum such as that required for Studio B would be difficult to qualify for, and probably not a very good way to use your money.

Business Loans

The business loan is usually a catch-22. You need the loan to start a business, but the bank won't give you a business loan until you've been in business successfully for several years. Most banks will not give start-up loans, and if they do, it's usually at a high interest rate, for a business that's almost certain to succeed.

If you've been in the music or audio business for a while, you may qualify for a business loan if you can convince the bank that this purchase makes good business sense. You may be asked to submit a five-year business plan outlining cost benefits, showing projected income and describing competition. Business loans usually offer good terms and reasonably low interest rates; however, the bank will probably want to monitor your business activities and your revenue statements.

Home Equity Loans

If you own your own home, this is the best bet for borrowing money. You can borrow up to a certain percentage of the equity in your home and use it for anything you want. The interest on this loan is tax-deductable, and if you wish, you can spread the loan out over a long period of time, keeping your payments low. Most banks have no prepayment penalties for this type of loan, should you want to repay the loan in less time. The drawback is that there will generally be closing costs associated. Be careful they don't rake you over the coals. Some institutions will charge points, or interest up front, payable as a deduction from the lump-sum check you receive at closing. The amount of money you actually receive could be considerably less than what you asked for!

Venture Capital

If you're planning on opening for business, there are private investment groups who sometimes make capital available for businesses that they feel are good investments. In return, they share in your profits. This should be a last resort, because what you are doing, in effect, with venture capitalists is taking on a slew of partners. Most venture capital schemes will require you to give them some say in how the business is run, which could get ugly if they don't see things the way you do.

Summary

As with the equipment list, you must be willing to make compromises when putting together a budget. How much quality will you sacrifice to cut costs? Also, don't give up so easily if the numbers won't work out for you. In a pinch, there are usually alternatives available to you, but you must be resourceful to find them. You may see a cable/connector assembly that you need advertised at a price well beyond your ability to pay. Chances are, an equally viable cable assembly can be built from individual parts for half the price if you're willing to take the time to search for them and do the work.

Many items are cheaper when purchased in bulk. Don't need so many of them? Check with others who might be interested in the same type of item and see if you can put together a joint order.

The budget is one aspect of studio design that you can expect to receive little help with from outside. Finances are a personal thing, and most people prefer to keep it that way. Equipment salespeople are certainly not going to go out of their way to keep your costs under control, so you've got to be thinking all the time. The main thing to remember is to be realistic, try to keep your emotions off the printed page, and pay attention to the seemingly minor items that can put you way over budget as you go along.

CONSTRUCTION: ACOUSTIC CONSIDERATIONS AND TECHNIQUES

This chapter touches on some of the unique construction designs that can be used in the home studio. Most of the construction work is typical of any home-improvement project, namely framing, insulating, and putting up Sheetrock or wallboard; and installing electrical outlets, plumbing fixtures, and lighting. There are only a few differences you need to concern yourself with, which deal with soundproofing, acoustics, and wiring.

If you're not doing the work yourself, keep a careful eye on the contractor you hire—be sure that the work is done in accordance with your specifications. Most building contractors have little understanding of the soundproofing requirements of a recording studio, and even if you explain in detail the kinds of things you want done, there may be a few corners that the builder thinks he can cut, which could compromise your design.

The Nature of Sound

Begin by looking at the way sound travels through space, and develop that knowledge into a basis for our construction designs. Sounds are variations in air pressure which move through the air at a specific rate of speed until they encounter a different type of surface or material. At this point, part of the sound wave's energy will be reflected by the surface, the rest will be absorbed by the material and dissipated in the form of heat, or emerge from the other side of the material in a subdued form. The ratio of deflected energy to absorbed energy differs from material to material. It would be nice if there were certain materials that were completely reflective or completely absorptive; however, there are no such examples in the real world.

Every time a sound travelling through one medium encounters another medium (a different material), part of it is reflected and part is absorbed. Therefore, the more materials a sound encounters on its journey from point A to point B, the less energy it will have on reaching its destination. This makes composite materials, such as plywood, or materials with internal air gaps good sound insulators.

Some materials, such as concrete, are extremely reflective. This is why your voice echoes noticeably in a parking garage. As you might guess, soft materials such as foam rubber or cotton are nonreflective, resulting in the "dead" or anechoic sound characteristics of a heavily carpeted room. Also, the mass of an object has an effect on its tendency to vibrate or resonate, with more massive objects being less likely to transmit sound.

Construction Materials

There are various types of materials and building supplies that come in handy in studio construction. Some are common; others you may have to do a little searching to find.

Weather Stripping

This material is resilient and is an excellent mechanism for acoustic dampening or sealing. It can be used to line doors and windows to provide a tight-fitting edge. It comes in various sizes and thicknesses and is relatively inexpensive.

Carpeting

Carpeting, as mentioned above, is extremely sound-absorbent. This is not always good, but in many situations you can take advantage of its characteristics. For example, the best way to resolve the problem of unwanted noise from an upper level (such as people walking and talking) is to carpet the upstairs floor. This will also help dampen the sound coming out of the studio into the upper levels. If you need to deaden certain frequencies in the studio or control room, carpet tiles placed at strategic intervals on the walls, floor or ceiling, or wall-to-wall carpeting on the floor may suit the purpose. Also, the foam padding that installers use beneath carpeting is inexpensive and works nicely as a sound deadener in some situations.

Acoustic Foam

For serious sound absorption, specially constructed foam panels can be purchased from several different manufacturers. They tend to be very expensive, ranging in price from $2 to $7 per square foot. They are secured to walls and ceilings with liquid adhesive, which adds to the overall cost. However, if you're having problems with reflections in the mid- to upper-frequency range, nothing beats it in terms of performance.

Wallboard

Standard gypsum panels (referred to as wallboard, Sheetrock, or gypsum board) both absorb and reflect sound. They come in 1/4-inch, 3/8-inch, 1/2-inch, 5/8-inch, and 3/4-inch thicknesses. If you're planning to do any soundproofing, thicknesses of less than 1/2-inch are only marginally effective. Panels can be doubled to achieve better performance.

Lumber

Wood is a rigid material and tends to vibrate and transmit sound. As you increase the mass of the wood, its sound transmission ability tends to decrease; therefore, two-by-four wall constructions are a little more sound-proof than two-by-three. Heavy plywood (1/2-inch or 3/4-inch) and particleboard (which is three times the mass of plywood) are both relatively good sound-stoppers.

Concrete

Concrete is great for soundproofing—nonhomogeneous, massive, reflective—but also expensive and difficult to work with. Cinder block and brick also make for very soundproof walls; however, they too are expensive and once they're up, they are not easy to tap into for wire routing and the like.

Concrete foundations tend to absorb moisture and can contribute to dampness in the studio. There are several excellent waterproofing/moisture barrier treatments that can be applied to concrete to cut down on this problem. Such treatment is highly recommended, especially if your studio will be located in a basement.

Fiberglass Insulation

Standard building insulation comes in various thicknesses and thermal ratings. Some types are faced with paper or foil, and others are unfaced. This material is a very good sound dampener, and makes quite a difference in the sound transmission of a wall when used. For isolating walls it is recommended that you use a minimum of six-inch-thick insulation throughout.

Wall Construction Techniques

Consider the effect of sound striking a standard wall construction consisting of two-by-four framing with insulation and Sheetrock (gypsum wallboard) on either side. Much of the sound energy is reflected back into the room, but some of it sets the wallboard vibrating. The vibration is transmitted to the framing, and subsequently to the wallboard on the opposite side. This wallboard becomes a mini-loudspeaker, transmitting a muted version of the original sound into the room on the other side. The two rooms on either side of this wall are acoustically coupled. This effect is further enhanced by the fact that the two wallboard surfaces are the same thickness, which means that they resonate at the same frequency.

Every rigid body has a resonant frequency. If you set it in motion at that frequency, it will continue to vibrate on its own for some time without any further stimulation. It likes that frequency. A tuning fork has a resonant frequency of 440 Hz. Flick it with your finger and it will vibrate happily, always at 440 Hz. A neat parlor trick is to get another 440-Hz tuning fork and hold it near, but not touching the one that's already in motion—both forks will soon be humming. This is the same effect that the wallboard on one side of the wall has on the wallboard opposite. If they're both of the same thickness, they'll both have similar resonant frequencies, and when one vibrates, so will the other.

By now it should be evident that this standard wall construction is not very soundproof. The amount of sound transmitted through this wall construction can be measured and described as its Sound Transmission

Coefficient, referred to as the STC. The wall described above probably exhibits an STC of about 35. For an isolating wall between a control room and studio area, the wall construction should be at least STC 50, preferably closer to STC 60. The remaining sections in this chapter will suggest ways to achieve an acceptable STC.

Soundproof Walls

One way to achieve this higher rating is to acoustically decouple the wall surfaces. There are two methods you can use. The best method is double-framing. You actually build two walls, with no contact between them. This is illustrated in Figure 4.1. Parallel-framed two-by-four studs are located one inch apart. One side is faced with two layers of 1/2-inch wallboard. The opposite side is faced with a single layer of 5/8-inch wallboard (to eliminate the resonant characteristic described above). A minimum of six inches of fiberglass insulation is used inside the wall.

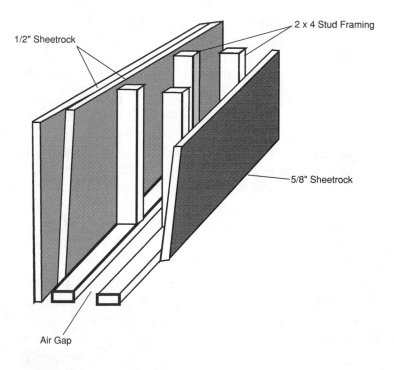

Figure 4.1   A double-framed wall.

Care should be taken not to introduce a common communication (a place where vibrations can move from one side of the wall to the other) at the points where the frames are secured to the floor and ceiling. If the floor is concrete and the studs are secured with nails or screws driven into the concrete, this is not a problem. If the floor is wood, however, it is possible to "short out" the wall—sound can be transmitted from one frame to the other across the wood floor. The same holds true for the ceiling. Be sure to nail the two frames to different ceiling joists if the joists·run parallel to the wall. You should be able to hit one of the vertical framing studs with a hammer, place your hand on the stud across from it, and feel little or no vibration. If you do feel significant vibration, it means there is communication between the two walls from either the ceiling or the floor. It may be necessary to add some caulking or resilient material to the place where the top beam of the frame meets the ceiling.

A less expensive but less effective way to decouple is the staggered-stud method. This method uses a single two-by-eight at the floor and ceiling, with studs located at opposite sides of the wall, staggered as shown in Figure 4.2 so that the wallboard on each side has its own set of studs. This wall should also be filled with a minimum of six inches of insulation, and fitted with different thicknesses of wallboard as described above.

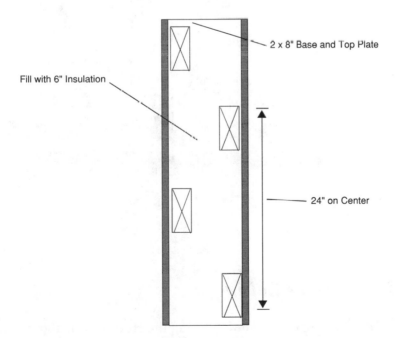

Figure 4.2 A staggered-stud wall.

If you can't (or won't) reframe any walls, but you need to increase the acoustic isolation of a room, you can do so by removing the wall surface and adding additional insulation to the wall, then installing resilient channels to the existing studs before mounting new Sheetrock. Resilient channels are metal tracks that hold a wall surface in position away from the surface it is attached to. They are designed to isolate the two surfaces so that the outer one will not pick up the vibrations of the inner surface.

Next, you must be sure that the room is acoustically sealed. If the wall has any kind of opening whatsoever, it will not be soundproof–just as a fish tank with even the smallest hole cannot hold water. Electrical outlets on opposite sides of the same wall, for example, cannot be located directly across from each other. Instead, they must be staggered, as shown in Figure 4.3. Once wired, the openings in the wall should be caulked and the outlet boxes themselves should be filled with acoustically absorbent material. Most hardware stores sell a sprayable foam insulation that serves this purpose well. After the wallboard is installed, acoustic sealant (silicone caulking) should be applied at all edges between walls, floor, and ceiling. The two rooms should be airtight.

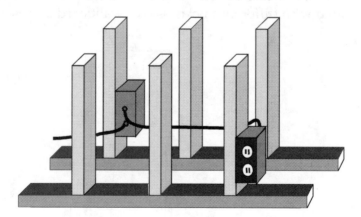

Figure 4.3 Staggered outlets

Soundproof Ceilings

To guard against sound entering the studio from above, the best thing to do is to install a multilayer cushion (consisting of hardboard, rubber, or foam underlay) and carpet on the upper floor (see Figure 4.4). This will deaden the sound of heavy footfalls and sharp raps.

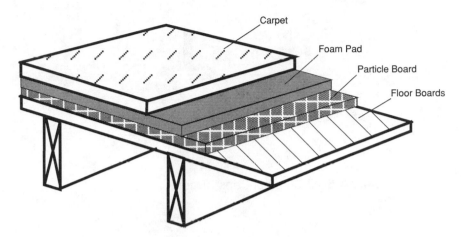

Figure 4.4 The floor treatment for the upper level.

Additional soundproofing can be achieved without breaking into the existing ceiling, by installing a new Sheetrock surface over the old, and sandwiching insulation between the two. This can be accomplished by using Z channels, as shown in Figure 4.5. Attach the Z channels across joists with 1 1/2-inch wallboard screws driven into the joists with a power drill. Orient the strips so that the flanges are all facing in the same direction. Raise the Sheetrock and attach it to the Z channel with 1-inch wallboard screws driven through the metal flange. Leave a 1/8-inch gap along the walls for caulking.

After completing one row of wallboard, slide 2-inch Styrofoam or fiberglass insulation between the wallboard and the ceiling above. At the last strip, glue the insulation to the Sheetrock and install.

A better way to insulate the ceiling is to remove the old Sheetrock, install 6-inch fiberglass insulation between the joists, screw in Z channels, and mount new Sheetrock.

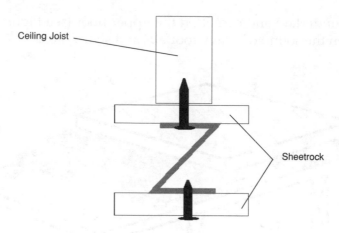

Figure 4.5   Z Channel Construction.

Soundproof Windows

One problem you've probably already thought of is that you might need to see from the control room into the studio. A window hole in a sound-proof wall is about as desirable as a skylight in a movie theater. From a soundproofing standpoint, the best way around this is to forget about a window. To cue a performer from the control room, do it audibly over the headphones, or install a small red light in the studio that can be activated from the console. If you must have visual contact, the next best solution is to install a camera in the studio and a monitor in the control room, and keep the isolating wall solid. If this is too expensive and/or impersonal for you, there is a way to construct a viewing window with an STC of about 55 for relatively little money. (I was able to do it for about $300.) Alternatively, you can purchase one of these windows prefabricated. They come in various sizes, but they tend to be expensive.

To build the homemade window, you first need to frame out the opening in both sides of the double wall. The window should be located at such a height that engineers seated at the console can easily see into the studio. Figures 4.6 and 4.7 are diagrams of the window construction, which consists of one plate of 1/4-inch leaded glass and another plate of 5/16-inch leaded glass, located on opposite sides of the framed wall. One of the panes is traditionally angled to cut down on glare. Contrary to popular belief, this angling has little effect on the sound transmission of the wall.

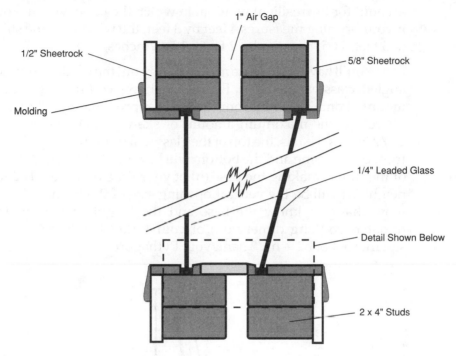

Figure 4.6   Window Construction.

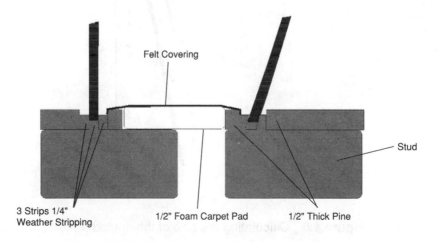

Figure 4.7   Detail of Window Construction.

Ask your local glass cutter to cut a pane for the straight side by measuring the opening of the frame minus 3/8 inch on height and 3/8 inch on the length. This is to allow 3/16 inch on the top, bottom, and sides to account for the resilient material in which the pane will sit. For example, if your opening measures 4 feet by 3 feet, the window pane should be cut to 3 feet, 11 5/8 inches by 2 feet, 11 5/8 inches.

You'll have to do some math to figure out the vertical dimension of the angled glass pane (sorry). Figure 4.8 shows you how. The pane will be mounted onto a two-by-four, which is approximately 3 1/2 inches wide. Therefore, the maximum amount of skew you should give it is about 2 1/2 inches. That is, the top of the glass will be mounted 1/2 inch from the front of the frame and the bottom will be mounted 1/2 inch from the back of the frame, making the base (b) of your little triangle 2 1/2 inches. The height (h) will be the vertical opening size of the frame minus 3/8 inch. Now that you know the base and the height, you need to find the hypotenuse (long dimension) of your little triangle, which will be the square root of b2 + h2. Thank you, Pythagorus.

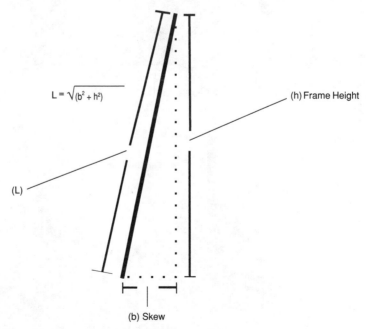

Figure 4.8   Calculating the size of the angled pane.

The first step in putting the double window together is to mount the straight pane. To do this, you screw on a piece of 1/2-inch-square pine at the base and top of the frame, which will become the inside brace. Also install pieces up each side. Line the entire square with 1/4-inch adhesive-backed weather stripping. Next, place another piece of weather stripping flat on the frame, where the window will sit, and go all the way around. You should now be able to press the pane into this brace, where it should sit rather snugly. To secure the pane, use 1/2-inch-thick pine, cut to fit from the pane to the outside edge of the wallboard. Line the wood with yet another piece of weather stripping, press it firmly against the window and screw it into the two-by-four. Do this on all four sides. The pane will be firmly seated and dampened from vibration by the weather stripping.

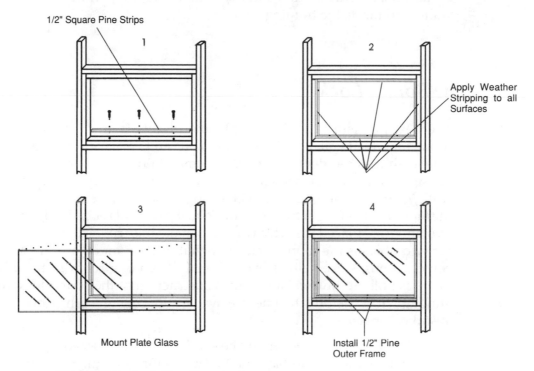

Figure 4.9 Installing the windowpane.

Before you install the other pane, line the inner perimeter of the window (the area in between the two panes) with foam rubber, which you can buy as squares of padding material from a carpet dealer. You don't want to have a rigid material (such as wood) lining the inside of the window, because it will allow sound pressure to build between the two panes. You can cover the ugly padding with some nice felt.

You still don't want to install the other pane until you clean, clean, clean the inside of both pieces of glass. Also, be sure to vacuum and wipe down the area between the panes. It is a good idea to give it a day or two for any particles to settle out, and then clean it again. Once you seal up that window, any dust and dirt that settles on the inside of the panes will require disassembly of the window to remove. You should leave the screws on one side of the window accessible so that the bracing and one pane can be removed for cleaning.

Repeat the process for the angled pane. Before adding molding around the outside of the window, caulk the entire perimeter where the wallboard meets the framing.

The Sound Lock

The next problem is getting people and objects from studio to control room, for which you need a doorway. You can't very well break a double wall with a single door and expect to maintain STC 60. You'll have to construct a sound lock, which works on the same principal as the double wall. Namely, sound has to travel through one wall, an inner space, and then another wall to get from the studio to the control room. In Figure 4.10, two doors are placed in such a way as to make this true. The area between the two doors is the sound lock. Note that walls A and B are single-wall constructions, since neither leads directly from one room to the other. There is nothing unusual about the construction of the sound lock area, although it is helpful to line the walls and ceiling with acoustically absorbent material.

The doors, however, should be solid—as massive as you can afford. The garden-variety, luan-faced hollow doors that you might buy for your bathroom are not enough to insulate against the din that will try to escape your studio as the bank of Mesa Boogie amplifiers begin to crank. I was able to find very heavy particle-board doors for about $80 apiece. I had to do the framing myself, which can be tough. Prehung doors are much easier, if you can find them at a good price.

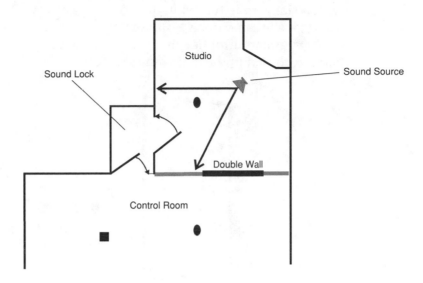

Figure 4.10 A sound lock.

Each door must achieve a tight seal when shut, and there are several ways in which to do this. Along the bottom of the door, you can install special weather stripping such as the types shown in Figure 4.11. The doorjamb bracing should be faced with weather stripping or some other absorbent material. Another possibility is to purchase the type of magnetic rubber seal that is found on refrigerator doors.

The Isolation Booth

The construction of the isolation booth will depend on the purpose for which it is intended. Ours was built into the studio area strictly to provide an acoustically "dead" space for voice-over work. It was not intended to sonically isolate a singer or instrument from the rest of the room (although it does a fairly good job of that in a pinch). In this case, single-stud construction was used, with a single-pane window and a normal door. The inside of the booth was carpeted to about three feet up the wall, and the remainder of the walls and the ceiling were treated with a commercial acoustic foam. If your budget allows, you can construct the isolation booth with a staggered-stud wall, double panes of glass in the window, and a heavy, well-sealed door. You can then use the room to isolate drums or to house a guitar amplifier that you don't want to leak into another track being recorded in the main studio area.

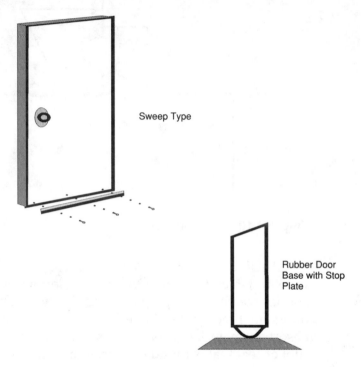

Sweep Type

Rubber Door Base with Stop Plate

Figure 4.11   Door treatments.

Wire Routing

Before closing up the walls with Sheetrock, you'll naturally want to route all electrical and audio wiring throughout the facility. It is very helpful to route plastic tubing in the walls and ceiling along the major routes that your audio wiring will travel. The audio wire can then be passed through this tubing, where it will be protected from sharp edges, nails, staples, screws, and any other menaces from the world of construction fasteners. Another advantage to this is that the wiring slides easily through the tubing. If, after the walls are completed, you find that a wire is damaged, replacing the wire is a simple matter of attaching a new wire to one end of the old one, then pulling on the other end until it is through. This method can be used even without the plastic raceways, but it is difficult because wires tend to get hung up on things like wood beams, lighting fixtures, and so on.

I'm going to go a little deeper into wiring in Chapter 6, but I'll start warning you now. Avoid routing audio wire close to power wire. If you must cross the path of a power conductor with a signal wire, cross it perpendicularly to the path of the power wire, and try to keep a few inches of space between them. Audio wires that run parallel to power conductors can easily pick up hum or some other unwanted interference which you'll spend half your life trying to track down after the walls are up.

Equipment Racks

It may be possible to save some money by mounting equipment racks directly into the walls. I did this in an area where there was three feet of space between the concrete foundation and the control room wall. Rack-mounting hardware can be purchased inexpensively from local audio dealers, and the length can be tailored to accommodate the amount of equipment you have. If your framing studs are located on 16-inch centers (standard building practice), you'll have to move the two studs where your equipment rack will be mounted. They will need to be 3 1/4 inches further apart to accommodate a rack for standard 19-inch equipment. You need to allow at least three feet of room behind the wall (some synthesizers and signal processing equipment measure more than two feet deep), and you need a way to get back behind the rack-mounted equipment.

If you are in a basement and you are not sure how good a moisture barrier you have between the foundation and the studio wall, you should put some plastic sheeting material in the opening between the concrete and the rack. This should also be done in areas where dust may be a concern (which is just about everywhere). Be careful, however, not to obstruct the flow of air over warm components. Power amplifiers and other equipment tend to run hot and need unrestricted airflow to survive without overheating. This is a special concern if you're mounting several power units on top of one another in a rack.

Climate Control

Sealing a room airtight is great for soundproofing but lousy for respiration and climate control. If you use air conditioning or forced hot air heating, you'll have air plenums (ductwork) running through the walls and or ceilings of your studio, delivering hot or cold air to the rooms. The motion of this air, coupled with the vibration of the hot or cold air source itself, creates noise which must somehow be minimized. Another problem is that both the studio and the control room may be fed by the same plenum, effectively creating a great big hole in your soundproof wall. Figure 4.12 shows a way to minimize this problem.

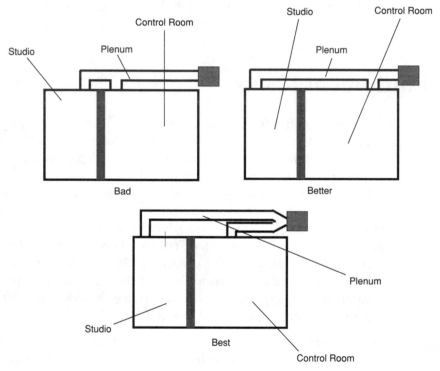

Figure 4.12 Ductwork configurations.

Most of the sound emanating from the air-conditioning ducts comes from turbulence created as the air flows through the plenum. This turbulence can be dampened by various mechanisms. The plenum can be lined with absorptive material, available through an air-conditioning supply. Baffles can also be placed in the plenum. Both methods greatly cut down on the high-frequency noise. Low-frequency noise, unfortunately, can only be attenuated by increasing the size of the plenum. It is better to try to cut down on low-frequency noise at the source, usually the air-conditioning or heat pump unit itself. Finally, the air velocity of the output duct should be limited to a maximum of 500 feet per minute to eliminate hissing at the exit grille.

If you cannot afford central air conditioning, it is possible to install room air conditioners in the studio. Be sure to "audition" the units at the dealer to be sure that they are relatively quiet machines. In most cases, you'll have to shut the units off for taping, and in some situations, the air-conditioner mounting may allow unwanted outside noise into the studio.

Other Considerations

Casement windows in a basement can be sealed against outside noise coming in and inside noise going out by constructing window plugs out of 3/4-inch particleboard. Layering the particleboard as shown in Figure 4.13 creates a well-performing sound barrier.

Before installing the Sheetrock walls of your studio, make sure that nothing in the walls or ceiling is able to vibrate and make noise. All pipes and lighting fixtures should be securely fastened and dampened with foam or insulation if necessary. We went as far as to line all the water pipes in the studio ceiling with wrap-around insulation. Check for leaks by running water through all the plumbing, and check the continuity of all wiring—audio and power.

Summary

It should be evident that there are no magic tricks and no overly complex or novel construction methods necessary to build a reasonably good project studio. It does take some attention to detail, and is a little more expensive than putting together a normal room of the same dimensions. It's also possible to modify existing structures to improve the quality of the room for recording purposes.

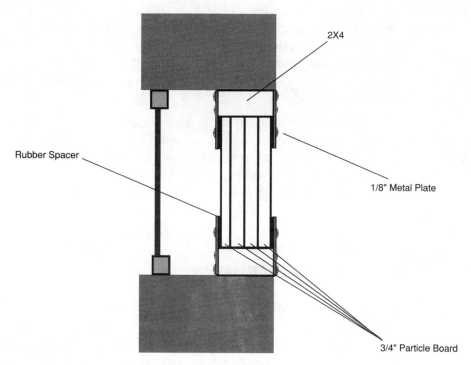

Figure 4.13   A seal for casement windows.

The main area of concern with regard to soundproofing is to acoustically seal all surfaces, and to use isolation methods such as double-wall construction and sound locks where possible. Before going ahead with construction, consider the concepts discussed in Chapter 7, "Acoustics," as these may have some bearing on the shape and placement of studio walls and other structures.

ELECTRICAL CIRCUITS: POWER AND AUDIO

Power Circuits

You've determined the layout of your studio. You have a good idea of what kind of equipment you're going to be using. Now, you need to determine how much electrical power the studio will require, and whether or not your existing electrical service can handle it.

In general, modern studio equipment does not draw much power. You might have to plug three or four digital signal processors into a circuit before you draw as much power as a single 100-watt light bulb. However, a typical studio incorporates a lot of devices, and some machines, such as open-reel multitrack tape decks and power amplifiers, do have moderately significant power requirements.

The key word here is *safety*. Improper power usage can result in a risk of fire or electric shock, so it's important to have an understanding of the basic household wiring system. If you're not well versed in electrical wiring, be sure to have all work done by a licensed electrician. If you do any wiring yourself, be certain that the work you're doing is in accordance with local electrical codes.

Figure 5.1 is a diagram of the power wiring connections in a typical room. The main power line enters the building and is connected to a box called the *entrance service panel*. One or more circuits lead from the entrance service panel into the room and terminate at the outlets. The same circuit(s) may also power the lighting fixtures, if any. At the service panel, the circuit is connected to a circuit breaker, which is supposed to disconnect power to the wiring in the event of an overload.

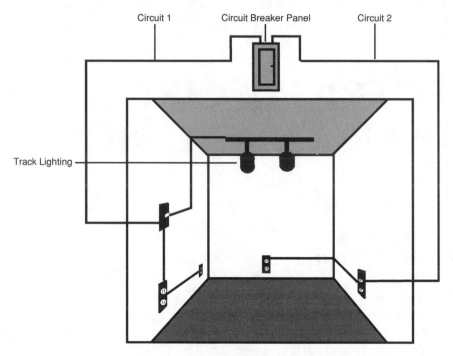

Figure 5.1   Power wiring in a small room.

Typical room circuit breakers are rated at 15 amps. If more than 15 amps flows through the wiring, the breaker trips and interrupts the circuit. This usually happens when Aunt Mabel connects a coffee machine to the same circuit that your wife is using to blow-dry her hair, right about the time that the deciding field goal of the Super Bowl is being kicked. You shouldn't get upset with the circuit breaker in this situation, because if it didn't trip, you might know the outcome of the Super Bowl, but the wiring in your walls would begin to smolder and eventually ignite, burning down the house.

Determining Requirements

There are two terms we need to discuss here. Power, which is measured in watts, and current, which is measured in amperes, or amps. All electrical devices will be marked with either a current rating or a power rating. You can get an idea of the number of amperes drawn by a 120-volt device by dividing its power (wattage) rating by 120. Therefore, a 60-watt light bulb draws about 0.5 amps (60/120 = 0.5).

In the example with Aunt Mabel, the blow dryer draws about 9 to 10 amperes of current. The coffee machine also draws close to 10 amperes in its brew cycle. By connecting the coffee machine, Aunt Mabel tried to pull 22 amperes from a circuit connected to a 15-amp breaker, which caused the breaker to trip immediately. If you load the breaker down gradually—piling on electronic devices, bringing the current draw to 14.5 amps, 14.75, 15.2, and so on—you might not trip the breaker. It could sit there at the edge of its trip threshold, while the household wiring runs uncomfortably hot.

To avoid this situation, you should assess your power requirements relative to the available outlets. Going back to the room in Figure 5.1, there are a total of four outlets, on two circuits. Two of the outlets are on circuit 1, and the other two are on circuit 2. Circuit 1 also feeds the track lighting in the ceiling. Each circuit is connected to its own 15-amp circuit breaker. Below is a list of equipment used in Studio A, and the power requirements of each device.

Table 5.1 Power requirements for the equipment in Studio A

Device	*Approximate Amperage*
Mixing board	2.0
8-track deck	3.0
MIDI workstation	1.5
Synchronizer	0.5
Cassette deck	1.0
Digital Signal Processor	0.5

continues

Table 5.1 Continued

Device	Approximate Amperage
Compressor/Limiter	0.5
Power amp	3.0
Total	**12.0**

You need about 12 amps to power the audio equipment. Circuit 2 alone is sufficient, and it is usually a good idea to power all the audio from a single circuit when possible. Therefore, you would plug the audio equipment into the two outlets connected to circuit 2, using multi-outlet strips.

As an aside, it's advisable to connect sensitive audio equipment (especially the digital stuff) through a surge suppressor. Choose a multi-outlet strip with surge suppression built in. This handy feature protects sensitive electronic circuitry from voltage spikes. Voltage spikes on house circuits are usually generated by lightning striking a nearby power line, although large motors turning on or off in the vicinity of the equipment can also generate spikes (an air conditioning compressor, for example).

Now, what if you need 25 amps in Studio A? It's not a good practice to run a circuit at its maximum—aside from the obvious danger, you could be plagued with nuisance tripping of the circuit breaker—so you'd plug a maximum of 14 amps into circuit 2, leaving 11 amps to feed into circuit 1.

Don't forget to calculate the power draw for the track lighting. The maximum bulb rating for each of the two lamps should be marked on the fixtures. When calculating, you must use this figure—rather than the rating of the bulbs in the fixture—because the bulbs may be of a lower wattage than the maximum. In this example, if the lamp fixtures are rated 150 watts each, you need 300 watts divided by 120 volts, or 2.5 amperes. The power draw for circuit 2 is then 13.5 amps, which is acceptable, but doesn't leave room for anything else you might want to add later, such as a space heater, a table lamp, or more equipment.

Separation of Circuits

For higher level projects such as Studio B, the ideal situation is to feed all audio circuits from a separate service panel. A separate panel can be electrically isolated from transient spikes and conducted noise emanating from oven thermostats, hair dryers, vacuum cleaners, and so on. These nasty things can cause all kinds of clicks, hums, and hisses in your audio path. The installation of an additional service panel must be done by a qualified electrician, and can cost from $900 to $2000 for a 100-amp service panel.

There are three main lines coming into a residential service panel, Line 1 (L1), Line 2 (L2) and Ground (G). As shown in Figure 5.2, the voltage from either Line 1 or Line 2 to ground is 120 volts. Each of these voltages represents a phase. Most audio equipment uses 120 volts, and would therefore be powered by circuits connected to one phase or the other. The voltage from L1 to L2 is 240 volts, and circuits used to power larger appliances such as electric stoves and clothes dryers would be connected to both phases. If it is not practical to use a separate service panel, it is helpful to connect all audio equipment circuits to one phase and all other studio power and lighting to the other phase. This will at least minimize the amount of line transients introduced to the audio path through power circuits.

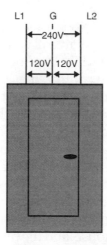

Figure 5.2   A residential service panel.

Grounding Power Circuits

If you don't know anything about electricity and don't care to learn, just remember this—electricity wants to find its way back to ground, and it will always choose the easiest path. If you generate some electricity and give it a fairly easy path to ground, it will light lamps, move speaker diaphragms back and forth, turn motors—it will do nearly anything you need.

Typical household wiring circuits consist of three identically sized wires. The hot wire, connected to Line 1 or Line 2 back the at the service panel, is your source of electricity. The neutral wire, connected to the service panel ground bus, is the intended path back to ground. The grounding wire (or, "safety ground") is also connected to the ground bus, and serves as a safety mechanism. It is intended to provide stray electricity with an easy path to ground (easier than, say, through your body) in the event of a fault in the equipment.

In a studio, the grounding wire serves an additional purpose. It provides an easy path to ground for electrical noise, which would otherwise find its way back through your audio circuits—no doubt stopping by your listening area to say hello. For this purpose, you want to make the grounding connections in your studio extremely easy paths for electricity to follow. Also, you must give it only *one* easy path to follow. If more than one direct connection to ground originates from a single point, you get what's known as a *ground loop*, which causes noise.

For a small studio with less than 20 power connections, the typical household wiring system will usually suffice. Some older houses are wired with 2-prong outlets that have no safety ground connections. For reasons of safety and noise control, these will have to be replaced with modern 3-prong outlets; the grounding terminals of the new outlets must be provided with a path to ground. This can be done by wiring the ground terminals of each outlet back to the ground bus at the service panel, or by routing the grounding wires to an 8-foot grounding rod. The grounding rod can be purchased at an electrical supply, and should be hammered into damp ground outside the building, near the electrical service entrance. Sometimes the grounding wires are connected to a conductive strap instead of a grounding rod; the strap is then fastened to a metallic cold water pipe in the house, and the pipe eventually goes back into the ground. This method is not, however, as reliable as the rod.

Standard household connections are daisy-chained; that is, the grounding terminal of outlet box C (see Figure 5.3) is connected to the grounding terminal of outlet box B, which is in turn connected to the grounding terminal of box A, and which is finally sent to the main grounding bus at the service panel. Every time you connect wire to a terminal, you introduce resistance, which means that it gets a little bit harder for electricity to pass through that connection. Electrical noise originating at outlet box A has a direct connection to ground; however, noise originating at outlet box C has a few terminal connections to go through, and might opt to take an easier route if it can find one.

To discourage this, it helps to wire direct ground connections from each outlet box (as shown in Figure 5.3b), using an insulated #10 AWG ground wire—which is easier if the studio walls are not up yet. If you do this, you must disconnect the ground wire that runs between the outlet boxes, or you will find yourself faced with the dreaded ground-loop situation. *Note:* Disconnecting the serial ground may violate local safety codes. Be sure to check with a qualified electrician before implementing different grounding schemes.

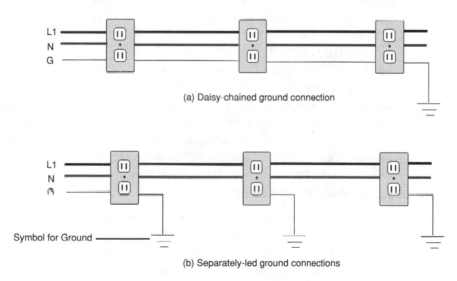

(a) Daisy-chained ground connection

(b) Separately-led ground connections

Figure 5.3 A daisy-chained outlet connection.

One last warning regarding grounding. The primary purpose of the ground connection is to protect the user of equipment against the risk of electric shock. Some magazine articles or other "authorities" may suggest that you simply disconnect the grounding pin on the plug of a device that is giving you ground-loop problems. Unless you provide some other means of grounding the unit, such as running a separate ground wire from the chassis of the device to the service panel ground, you are placing the user in a dangerous situation. Chapter 9 discusses troubleshooting ground loops and shows ways of defeating annoying ground loops and other noise problems without compromising the level of safety in your studio.

Lighting

There are three different types of lighting that can be used in the studio: recessed ceiling fixtures (sometimes called *hi-hats*), track lighting, and separate plug-in-type lamps. Never use fluorescent lighting in a studio–flourescent fixtures are likely to induce noise onto your powerlines, which could get back into your audio circuits. You should try to create a comfortable, diffuse lighting situation without using dimmers, if possible. Lighting dimmers chop up the AC power waveform, and radiate radio frequency (RF) noise into other electrical circuits. Some of the more expensive dimmers are RF protected; however, when spotlight-type bulbs are dimmed, the elements in the bulbs themselves will sometimes rattle and make noise! There is no way to know whether this will happen until you actually install the lighting system. If you find that you need more subdued lighting in the studio, get lower-wattage bulbs. Another alternative is to install two or more light switches, so that individual fixtures can be turned on and off as needed.

Track lighting is attractive and effective, and can be directed wherever you need to focus. The only drawback is that it requires some extra ceiling height. If you have low ceilings, it is better to install recessed lighting, which can also be directed through the use of special cover fixtures. Be sure to buy fixtures that are specially rated to be installed in contact with insulation. Most recessed lighting fixtures require that insulation be kept a minimum of six inches from the metal enclosure; however, this is less than ideal for your soundproofing efforts. The specially rated hi-hats are not more expensive than the regular ones, but they may be more difficult to find.

Other Considerations

When having the electrical circuits installed, be sure to indicate to the electrician what each circuit will be used for. Circuits intended for air conditioning or other heavy-load applications will need more heavy-duty wiring, switching, and circuit breakers. In areas where you need many outlets, special outlet strips are available that can be installed in the wall by the electrician.

Another investment which may save lots of headaches is a power-line conditioner (see Figure 5.4). These devices (many of them rack-mounted for convenience) have multiple outlets into which you plug your audio equipment. The conditioner constantly monitors the line voltage and adjusts for any abnormalities. Power surges are *clamped* (that is, excessive voltage is diverted away from the equipment to protect it); *brownout* voltages (when the power company temporarily cannot deliver full voltage) are brought up to operating level. Entire sessions can be ruined by a single voltage fluctuation. These fluctuations do not always originate at the power company. Some heavy current devices in your home—such as the refrigerator, oil burner, or air conditioner—can cause severe drops in voltage when they turn on.

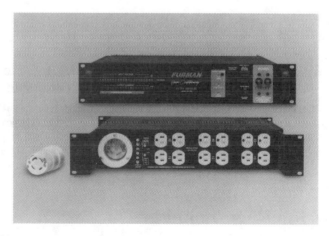

Figure 5.4 The Furman Power Conditioner.

Audio Circuits

In any studio, the main thing to remember is to try to keep all audio cable runs short—10 feet or less is optimal. This may not be possible in a larger studio, where other methods may be needed to counteract the ill effects of long cable runs, but it is usually possible in small, single-room setups. Short cable runs will cut down on the amount of hum or RF noise introduced into the signal path, and will reduce the possibility of high-frequency loss in the audio path. Locate tape machines and outboard equipment as close to the mixer as possible, and connect the power lines of all this equipment to outlets fed by the same circuit breaker. Always use the highest quality audio cables you can afford, preferably braided-shield cable with metal connector housings.

In a larger studio, planning and implementing the audio wiring scheme is one of the most critical tasks. Most of the signal-wire routing takes place immediately after the framing has been done, before filling walls and ceilings with insulation and putting up Sheetrock. Install the power wiring first, keeping in mind areas where audio wire will be routed. Try to leave plenty of berth for the audio wiring to travel without coming within 12 inches of the power lines. This is especially true for speaker wires.

Where this is not possible, be sure to cross the audio and power lines at right angles to each other (this reduces the amount of audio wire exposed to the electromagnetic field of the power wiring). Never run signal wire and power wire together side by side, or through the same wire-routing system. It is also beneficial to route line-level and mike-level cables separately, and if you use any digital transmission lines (these generate lots of high-frequency hash!), route them away from the audio wiring and keep the cables short.

Wiring Requirements

When laying out the studio wiring, try to anticipate the needs of the musicians and engineers using the equipment. If a band is recording in the talent area, each player will need to have some connection to the console, through either a microphone or a direct line input. Each will also need a headphone or cue mix for monitoring while recording. For these purposes, stations are installed in the studio area in convenient locations around the room. Each of these stations may house some combination of microphone, line-level, and headphone jacks.

The engineer will need access to signals coming from the tape deck area, the MIDI setup, the live instruments, and the outboard processing equipment. He or she should be able to route each and every signal to the console input of choice without difficulty. This kind of routing control is provided by a patch bay, which is essentially a bank of interconnections to which nearly all audio wiring in a studio is led. Patch bay design is extremely important and somewhat complex, so I have devoted a separate chapter to it.

Figure 5.5 is a diagram of the wiring layout for Studio B. The talent room contains four stations and the isolation booth contains 1 station. The station closest to where the drums would be situated contains six microphone inputs, one line input and one headphone output. Along the front wall are three stations, each with one microphone input, one line input and two headphone outputs. In the isolation booth, the main microphone input is wired directly to the console and there is a station containing three headphone outputs plus two additional microphone inputs. Total audio runs for the studio wiring are 12 mike-level wires, four line-level wires and 10 headphone wires.

The console has 32 balanced microphone inputs, and only 12 were needed, so frequent patching or rerouting of those inputs was not anticipated. As a result, the microphone wires from the studio were led directly to the console, without going to the patch bay.

In the control room, a few hundred line-level signal connections are led to and from the patch bay. These include audio signal wires from the synthesizers and MIDI sound generators, audio connections from the outboard equipment and mixdown machines, tape sends and tape returns from the multitrack, and all console line-level inputs and outputs. Figure 5.6 is a block diagram of these connections. Since raising the floors was not possible in this room, all audio wiring is routed through the walls and ceilings. The patch bay is mounted into the control room wall near the console, and access to the area behind the bay is provided through removable wall panels in the control room.

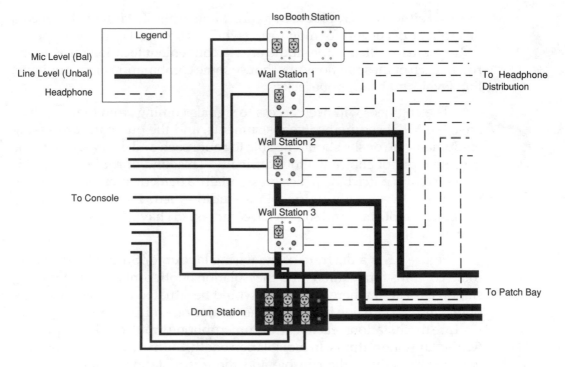

Figure 5.5 The wiring layout for the Studio B talent room.

If necessary, audio wiring can be routed, concealed, and kept out of harm's way without breaking into the walls and ceilings. This can be accomplished by using galvanized steel (or plastic) moldings available through electrical or audio supply stores. These cable troughs, each capable of routing many wires, are provided with convenient means to mount them to walls or ceilings. They come in a variety of colors, are inexpensive (less than $1 per foot), and are easy to install.

Balanced versus Unbalanced Wiring

Unfortunately, electromagnetic energy given off by power lines, amplifiers, digital equipment, and a bunch of other "bad guys" can (and will) be picked up by a length of metal wire–similar to the way an antenna can pick up radio signals.

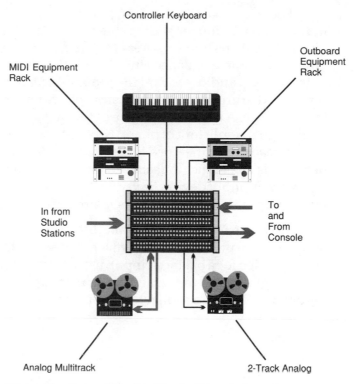

Figure 5.6   The wiring layout for the Studio B control room.

This shows up as a voltage referenced to ground. Consequently it is interpreted as an audio signal by the input device and ends up amplified as hum or noise in the music program. To counteract this problem, signal wire is usually shielded. A metal covering (sometimes foil, sometimes braided wire) is wrapped around the wires inside the cable, and one (or both) of the ends is connected to ground. The stray signals are picked up by the shield and dumped to ground before they can get to the signal wire. This works fine for short distances, but it's not always effective enough for longer cable runs.

The use of balanced wiring (wherever possible) will help eliminate induced hum in longer audio cable runs (more than ten feet); it will also give a benefit on short runs near magnetically "noisy" equipment. This is how it works: an unbalanced input reads the difference in voltage between a single "hot" audio lead and the grounded lead. In this case, any voltage referenced to ground (including stray electromagnetic noise) is amplified by the device. A balanced input uses two hot leads and a ground lead. The audio signal is split (out of phase) between the two hot leads, and the input device reads the difference in voltage between them. Since electromagnetic fields will induce the same voltage on both hot wires, it is read as zero signal by the input device. Pretty neat. The problem is that this only works on devices with balanced inputs fed from balanced outputs.

Most instrument outputs (amplifier direct outs, synthesizer outputs, and so on) are unbalanced. However, if the signal has a long way to travel and is headed for a balanced input, it can be converted to a balanced signal at the beginning of the cable run by using a balancing transformer (see Figure 5.7). They are available from professional audio supply stores.

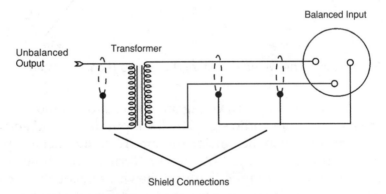

Figure 5.7   A circuit diagram of a balancing transformer.

Types of Wire

Wiring all of these connections requires an awful lot of cable. 22-gauge general-use shielded signal cable is available in 1000-foot reels for about $.08 to $.10 per foot. This is the cheap stuff, but it works. It contains three separately insulated stranded leads for balanced connections and a foil shield. The jacket is flame-rated in accordance with the National Electrical Code. This can be used for all signal-level studio wiring. Manufacturers of this cable include Gepco, Belden and Canare.

If you can afford better stuff, such as top-of-the-line cables by Canare or Mogami, by all means use it—it will increase the quality of your audio signal paths. For headphone output connections, use a minimum of 18-gauge speaker wire or lamp cord (sometimes called *zip cord*), available at any hardware store. For speaker connections, use only 10- to 14-gauge stranded wire.

For unbeatable signal transmission and noise rejection, there are special cable assemblies that can be purchased from companies such as Monster Cable. These are expensive, heavily shielded, heavy-gauge cables and connectors built specifically for professional recording applications. If your budget allows, I recommend using such an assembly for the interconnections between the multitrack and the console.

Labelling

Great care should be taken to label all wires as you route them. Numbered adhesive labels can be purchased from an audio supply, and should be of a quality that will last for many years without detaching from the wire. Be sure to attach the wire label at both ends of the cable, not more than three inches from the end of the wire. Make a list of all wiring and corresponding label numbers and put it in a safe place.

Studio Input Stations

For Studio B, each of the studio input stations was custom made using ordinary electrical-supply items. Figure 5.8 shows the construction of one of three identical stations along the front wall.

Figure 5.8 A wall station in Studio B.

It consists of a standard plastic wiring box (using plastic boxes eliminates one more possible source of ground loops), a blank plastic outlet cover, three 1/4-inch stereo input jacks, and one XLR input jack. To mount the 1/4-inch input jacks, drill a 5/16-inch hole in the outlet cover and secure the jack with its locknut.

The XLR jack is a little trickier. This connector is round (roughly 1/2 inch in diameter), with a small ridge on the upper side for positioning. Use a 1/2-inch metal hole punch (available in hardware stores or electronic supply houses), and then file out a small opening for the ridge. Two small holes must be drilled directly above the 1/2-inch opening to accommodate the XLR's mounting screws.

Solder connections to the jacks in each station should be done last, after all major construction work is complete. Be sure to clean the stations thoroughly, removing dust and construction debris, and use the proper soldering techniques as explained in Chapter 6.

The other station panels (such as those shown in Figure 5.9) are different in layout, but constructed in much the same manner. As an alternative, premounted XLR and 1/4-inch panels are available through professional audio supply stores and by mail order.

Figure 5.9 Isolation booth wall stations.

How to Construct a Headphone Distribution System

The musicians in the studio will usually be cued via headphones. This means that each musician must have a station available to plug in headphones, and those headphones must be supplied with an amplified cue mix from the console. There are a number of four- and six-station headphone amplifiers available on the market, ranging in price from $300 to $500. Most of them are rack-mount devices with left and right inputs, plus four to six output jacks mounted to the front panel, each with a separate volume control. These are great for small studio setups, where several musicians using the same cue mix will be located in a small area.

There is a disadvantage to this type of setup in a larger studio. Because all the headphone outputs originate from the same place, it can get messy when you have a full band trying to plug themselves into the thing. As an alternative, you can construct your own headphone distribution system, using a small 50- to 70-watt amplifier and a terminal block to send cue mix signals to the various stations in the talent room. You can even set it up so that two different cue mixes can be sent to the same room.

Studio B's console has four effect sends and returns plus four auxiliary bus sends and returns. I chose to use auxiliary sends A and B as the left and right headphone cue mix sends. The Auxiliary A and B outputs lead to a small 70-watt amplifier. The amplifier speaker outputs are connected to a small screw-type terminal block, and then distributed as shown in Figure 5.10. In the talent area, there are a total of 10 headphone jacks. Seven of these jacks receive a stereo mix with the Aux A send as the left channel and the Aux B send as the right channel. The other three jacks are connected as mono cues with both channels fed by the Aux A signal.

This is an advantage in a situation where one or more of the players wants to hear a particular instrument in their headphones while the others do not. For example, a drummer adding tracks might not want to hear previously recorded percussion tracks, but the guitarist might. You would send the percussion tracks to the Aux B output, so they show up in the right channel of the stereo headphone jack. Send the rest of the mix to both Aux A and B outputs. If the drummer plugs into a mono headphone jack, fed only by Aux A, he would not hear any of the percussion tracks. If you want to get fancy, you can install a potentiometer (volume control) into each station to regulate signal level.

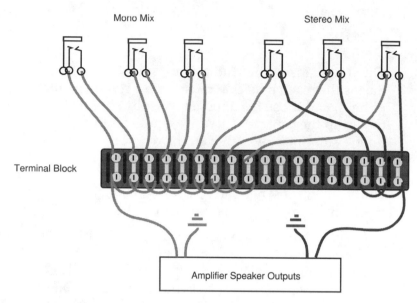

Figure 5.10 Headphone distribution for Studio B.

The total cost for the headphone amplifier/distribution system for Studio B was $180.00.

Other Circuits

Telephone, cable TV, FM and TV antenna, and alarm-system wiring should be installed before completing wall construction. Even if your budget doesn't allow the purchase of some or all of these things, it can save you time and money later if you install the wiring at this time, and everything ends up being much neater as well.

Summary

Your main concern with electrical circuits is safety. Be sure to consult a qualified electrician before making any modifications to the electrical system. In a small studio, be careful not to overload circuits with too much equipment. For larger studios with considerable power requirements, try to keep audio power circuits isolated from other major power connections at the service panel. Be sure all grounds are intact and avoid ground loops.

Route all audio circuits away from power circuits. Separate different types of signal wires (digital and analog). Wherever possible, use short signal runs and/or balanced wiring connections. Keep all wiring away from traffic areas and be sure to label all cables carefully.

6

THE AUDIO PATCH BAY

If the mixing console is the brains of the recording studio, the patch bay (see Figure 6.1) is the spinal cord, serving as a crossroads and a pathway for all signals to be routed into the body of the facility. There is no greater hindrance to creativity and productivity in a studio than an inadequate patching system. This applies even to smaller setups.

Figure 6.1   The Furman PB-40 patch bay.

The *patch bay* is a system of jacks mounted in a panel, which can be linked together using patch cords (the way an old-time telephone operator linked calling parties). It allows you to quickly connect the inputs and outputs of any device to the inputs and outputs of any other device. Should you decide that the background vocals need compression, you can easily route the mixer channels for the background vocals to the compressor

115

input. If you want to plug the keyboard into a mixer channel, you can do it at the bay, instead of running around to the back of the console and fooling with an obtrusive mass of board connections.

Patch bays come in several shapes and sizes. Some professional or semiprofessional consoles have prewired patch bays built into the desk. If you're fortunate enough to get a board with an integral patch bay, it will alleviate nearly half the studio wiring work. Stand-alone patch bays come in rack-mountable panels. The front of the bay contains open jacks which may be either bantam or 1/4-inch. The type you choose is usually dependent on the amount of space you have.

Bantam connectors are much smaller than 1/4-inch (52 1/4-inch jacks can be mounted into a single rack-space panel, as opposed to approximately 96 bantam jacks in the same space). As a result, a bantam patch bay can be constructed in half the rack space that a 1/4-inch bay would use. The tradeoff (there is always a tradeoff) is that bantam bays and plugs are a little more expensive than 1/4-inch, they tend to be a little less rugged, and the smaller bay jacks are more difficult to wire.

The rear of the unit can be equipped either with jacks (of any common audio type), or with solder terminals for direct wiring connections. For small studios like Studio A, it doesn't always pay to set up a permanent bay; in that case a rear panel jack configuration would make sense. For larger applications it is both cheaper and more reliable to solder the rear connections.

Patch Bay Types

There are four different patch bay wiring configurations, and these are shown in Figure 6.2. The configurations correspond to the way the jacks and terminals are internally connected. In every configuration, the upper rear jack or terminal is wired to the upper-front jack and the lower-rear jack or terminal is wired to the lower-front jack.

The simplest (and most commonly used) arrangement is the open configuration, where none of the upper jacks are connected to lower jacks. In this mode, you could connect the inputs of some outboard unit (such as reverb) to the upper rear connections, and the outputs to the lower rear connections. At the front of the panel, the reverb inputs and outputs are conveniently accessible.

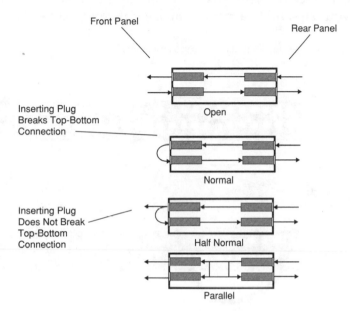

Figure 6.2   Patch bay wiring configurations.

The next type of connection is the *normal* configuration. In this arrangement, with nothing plugged into the front panel jacks, the signal flows from the top to the bottom. Usually, multitrack tape sends (inputs) are *normalled* to the console bus outputs. with no plugs inserted into the patch bay, the signal flows from the bus output to the tape input. To route something other than the console bus output to the tape input, a plug is inserted into the front panel which breaks the normal top to bottom connection. This configuration can be used to connect any two devices (or input/output pairs) that will be connected during the majority of studio operations.

Figure 6.3 is a diagram of one section of the Studio B patch bay. The first eight upper-row jacks are connected to the mixer subgroup outputs. Below them are the 16 multitrack *tape sends* (inputs). The mixer subgroups are normalled to the first eight tape sends; therefore a signal sent to subgroup output 1 always shows up at input 1 on the multitrack. To send signals to multitrack inputs 9 through 16, insert a patch cord into subgroup output 1 and send it to tape send 9, and so on. In this manner you can easily do sixteen-track recording using an "eight-out" mixer. The only limitation is that you can send to a maximum of eight tape channels at any one time.

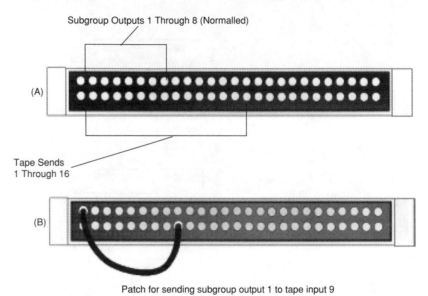

Figure 6.3 Layout for a tape-send patch.

Also, tape deck outputs are usually normalled to the console tape inputs. In my studio, the most commonly used signal processing devices are normalled to the console effects sends and returns.

The *half-normal* configuration is exactly the same as the normal configuration, except that inserting a plug in the front panel output jack does *not* break the normal top-to-bottom signal flow. This allows you to split the signal into two paths, one exiting at the lower rear jack, the other exiting at the front jack where the patch cable is inserted. This situation is known as a *mult*, short for *multiple*, because there are multiple identical signals from a single input.

The last configuration is the *parallel* configuration, in which a signal appearing at the upper rear jack will be split into a three-way mult. This is great for routing the same signal to three different mixdown decks, for example.

Patch bays fitted with jacks on front and back are usually wired for a specified configuration at the factory. You must indicate whether you want an open, normal, half-normal, or parallel configuration at the time of purchase.

Jacks come in two- or three-contact versions. The *two-contact* version is the typical mono jack used in unbalanced audio equipment, such as guitar inputs. There is a tip connection which is used for signal (hot), and a sleeve connection used for ground. *Three-contact*, or stereo, jacks have a tip connection, another connection a little further back (called the *ring* connection) and a sleeve connection. This type of jack is used for stereo headphone inputs and for balanced connections where tip is the signal (or "+"), ring is return (or "−") and sleeve is ground. Diagrams for each jack are shown in Figure 6.4.

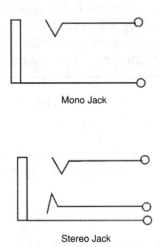

Mono Jack

Stereo Jack

Figure 6.4   Mono and stereo jack diagrams.

On patch bays with solder terminations on the rear panel, the configurations depend on the connections made. The jacks on a normalling patch bay have additional pins for the purpose of normalling. There is a pin for normalling the tip and one for the ring, as shown in Figure 6.5. To normal a jack pair together, solder a wire from the normalling pin on one jack to the normalling pin of the same type on any other jack. This allows you to normal any two jacks together, regardless of their relative positions on the patch bay. Leaving the normalling pins open would result in an open configuration.

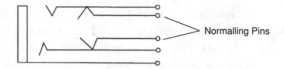

Figure 6.5   Stereo Jack with Normalling Pins.

One of the problems associated with patch bay design is the potential of creating ground loops through a variety of patch configurations. A common example occurs when patching into normalled jacks. Since the sleeve connection (ground) does not have a normalling pin—and so is not broken when a plug is inserted in the jack—a ground loop is often created. The solution lies in coming up with a consistent grounding scheme for the cable shields at the patch bay—which can be tricky, depending on how your bay is set up.

When laying out the bay, try drawing different patch setups, tracing the circuit path, and trying to pinpoint possible ground loops that could be created. If solutions become difficult to find, a good reference is Phillip Giddings' *Audio System Design and Installation*; it goes into great detail on the nuances of grounding and interconnection.

Laying Out the Patch Bay

Before configuring the patch bay and determining the number of open, normal, half-normal, and parallel jacks that will be needed, a complete knowledge of all equipment inputs and outputs must be assembled. It is also necessary to leave room in the bay for expansion in anticipation of adding new equipment to the studio at a later date. This is where your knowledge of the recording process—as well as your sense of purpose and future direction for the studio—will be especially important. Of course, the connections to the bay can be modified later, but if you're well prepared, changes can be minimized.

It's a good bet you will want to send quite a few of the inputs and outputs from the console to the patch bay. Once a mixing console is chosen, get a drawing or photograph of the rear panel input and output jacks. When setting up the bay, the operating manual for the console (if you can obtain it) is invaluable in the process of determining the exact function of each jack, which inputs/outputs are balanced and which are not, and the line levels at every point. A single mixer channel may have some or all of the following possible input/output types:

Low Impedance Mic Input Balanced input for use with low-impedance microphones or low-level sources equipped with an XLR connector.

Line Input Input for line level signals, usually balanced. Typical nominal input level is –10 to +4 dbv.

Tape Input Input for use with tape sources, usually balanced. Nominal input level –10 to +4dbv.

Direct Out Pre-EQ/fader output for splitting the input signal to allow routing to a separate input or device.

Insert or Pre-Patch Send Unbalanced output for sending pre-EQ/fader signal to an outside source (such as an effects processor) or another input channel. Inserting a jack into this output breaks the input signal on some mixers—in which case it is necessary to normal the other end of the cable to a return, so that signal can be run through the input channel when the insert send is not in use.

Insert or Pre-Patch Return Unbalanced input for return of the above signal.

Post-Patch Send Unbalanced output for sending post-EQ/fader signal to an outside processing source. As in the case of the pre-patch send, inserting a jack in this input may break the signal path for the input channel.

Post-Patch Return Unbalanced return input for above signal.

On a 32-input board, therefore, it is possible to have 224 (32×7) patch bay points taken up by the input channels alone. In addition, there are the subgroup channels, monitor channels and the master section containing input and output points for sends and returns, all auxiliary bus sends and returns, effects sends and returns, and more.

Figure 6.6 shows the complete layout of the Studio B patch bay with all normal connections marked. Notice that several mults were included for situations where signals might need to be split and run to several devices, or where several signals might be sent to a single input.

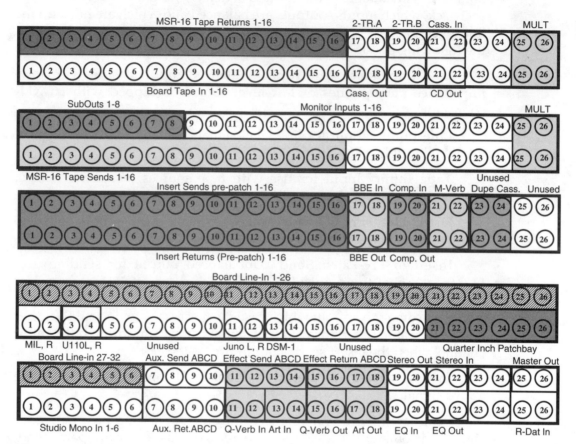

Figure 6.6 Studio B patch bay layout.

Looking at this layout, some audio professionals may question the wisdom of bringing so many wires to the patch bay. Since patch bays (especially incorrectly wired patch bays) are great collectors of unwanted electrical noise, and also generally increase the length of signal paths for any devices connected to them, many system designers prefer to keep patch bay connections to a bare minimum. Again, there is a tradeoff; in the end, the decision is best left to the designer. Being a musician—and one who hates to change cables and reroute wires—I am a member of the "bring-it-all-to-the-patch-bay" school of design, and I'm willing to take my chances with electromagnetic noise.

If you need to conserve patch bay space (or patch bay expense), you can skip some of the less commonly used channel jacks. I opted not to send the console post-patch sends and returns to the bay. The reason for this was twofold. First, I felt that the need to process post-fader, post-EQ signals was minimal. Second, a jack in the output plug would break the channel signal path, requiring the signal to be routed to the patch bay and then normalled back to the post-patch return. This represented an additional 30 feet of unbalanced wire run for any signal sent to the board inputs. I already had a 30-foot run being used for the pre-patch sends and returns, and did not want to increase it to 60 feet.

For the 260-point patch bay of Studio B, five ADC 1/4-inch, hard-wired bays were used, 52 jacks per bay. I had a clear idea of the kind of work I would be doing most of the time in the studio, so I tried to wire the patch bay so as to require the least amount of patching for normal operating conditions. This was done by normalling frequently used instrument outputs to board channel inputs, and normalling the inputs and outputs of certain signal-processor effects to the effects send and return buses.

There are studio designers and recording engineers that frown on all this normalling; having many devices normalled or half-normalled into the signal paths leads to a slightly greater complexity of patchwork, should those devices be needed for other uses. Often, patch bays will be laid out with all inputs in one area and all outputs in another—creating a more recognizable and (to some) a more user-friendly pattern.

Cost

When budgeting, we included the cost of all station inputs, audio wiring, connectors and patch bay units as part of the overall patch bay cost. Table 6.1 shows how it broke down for Studio B:

Table 6.1 Cost breakdown for the Studio B patch bay

Item	Quantity	Unit Cost	Total
ADC Patch bays	5	$159.00	$ 795.00
Hook-up wire	5000 feet	0.08	400.00
RCA Plugs	32	1.80	57.60
XLR Male Plugs	12	2.20	26.40
XLR Female Jacks	11	3.25	35.75
1/4 in. Stereo Plugs	150	2.00	300.00
1/4 in. Mono Plugs	30	2.00	60.00
1/4 in. Stereo Jacks	14	2.00	28.00
1/4 in. Mono Jacks	4	2.00	8.00
XLR Panel Mount Jacks	11	3.00	33.00
Outlet Boxes	7	3.00	21.00
Teflon Tubing	30 feet	10.00	10.00
Shrink Tubing	10 feet	20.00	20.00
Solder	2 Rolls	5.00	10.00
Labels	400	0.02	8.00
Total			**$1812.75**

To purchase a prewired patch bay or to have a subcontractor design and build a 260-point bay would cost more than twice that amount, so if you can do the work yourself, you can save a lot of money. It is time-consuming work, however, and requires a good deal of patience. Each patch bay connection must be properly dressed and soldered (as explained below) and each wire must by securely terminated by a connector. This represents many hours of repetitive work, but the satisfaction of having designed and constructed a functioning system is well worth it.

Soldering

Good soldering practice is an art, requiring strict adherence to procedure. In my experience, nearly half the equipment problems and connection failures in the studio can be traced to bad solder connections, so it pays to be diligent when making the original connections.

Soldering Tools

An obvious first step is to procure a good soldering iron. For patch bay and audio connections, an iron rated approximately 35 watts works well. Some soldering irons have adjustable wattage outputs, which is convenient if you expect to be doing different types of soldering (such as sensitive electronic circuit-board repair, as well as larger wiring jobs). Do not attempt to use a high-capacity soldering iron or magnetic-field-type iron (soldering gun) on electronic circuits. For work on integrated circuits, the soldering iron should have an isolating transformer to guard against the possibility of damage to the ICs through static discharge. Some of the less expensive irons have a tendency to heat up in your hand, becoming very uncomfortable (and perhaps even unusable) for longer jobs.

After purchasing a new iron, it is necessary to *tin* the tip of the iron. Let the iron heat up for about a minute, and then apply solder to it, covering the entire tip. Let that sit for another minute, and wipe off the solder with a damp sponge. This procedure coats the surface of the tip and reduces the tendency of solder to roll off the tip of the iron while you are working.

You'll also need some type of *desoldering* device to correct mistakes. There are two popular desoldering methods. One is to use a solder-sucker or *solderpullit*, which is a spring-loaded mechanism that sucks molten solder from a surface using a vacuum action. The other is *solder wick*, which is a braided wire that can be heated up and applied to the solder. The hot braid draws the solder up and away from the work surface.

Soldering a wire to a connector requires four hands, leaving most of us about two hands short. A flexible *soldering vise* is extremely useful to make up for this deficiency. This is a contraption consisting of two or more alligator clips mounted to flexible arms. The two clips can be positioned in almost any direction, and can be made to hold a wire and a connector together, leaving your hands free to apply heat and solder.

Use only 60/40 Tin/Lead (SnPb) rosin-core solder. It comes in various thicknesses, and the thickness you use will depend on your personal preference and the nature of the work. You will also need a good set of wire strippers, needle-nose pliers, scissors, a utility knife, diagonal wire cutters, a sponge (to clean the iron tip), and a holder for the iron. A magnifying glass helps for examining solder joints.

Soldering Techniques

Always wear safety glasses while soldering. Molten metal spitting up off of an iron into your eyeballs really hurts.

Before soldering *anything*, make sure both surfaces are clean and free from dust, dirt, rust, oil, grease, tarnish, or any other foreign substance.

The majority of connection work done in the studio involves soldering one or more stranded copper wires to a terminal or connector. Before making any connections, the wire must first be *dressed* and *tinned*. Most of the time you'll be working with audio cable consisting of three wires and a ground shield or braid. To dress the wire, strip back the outer jacket about 1 1/2 inches. Unravel the metallic braid, and twist it together to form a sort of stranded wire. Next, strip approximately 1/2 inch of insulation from each of the stranded conductors. It is a good idea to buy some Teflon tubing (sometimes known as *spaghetti*), slightly larger than the inner conductors, to apply to them as supplementary insulation. For 22 AWG conductor, use 3/64-inch. (1.2mm) tubing. Next, cut a one-inch piece of heat-shrink tubing, and slip it over the cable end as shown in Figure 6.7.

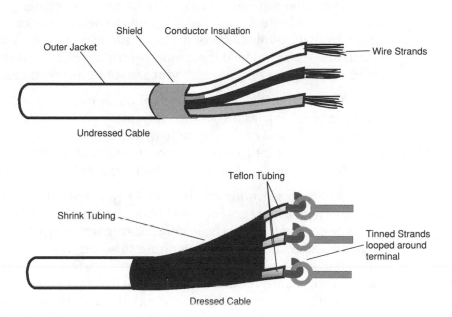

Figure 6.7 A dressed connection.

To tin each conductor, first twist the strands together. Heat the wire with the soldering iron, and then apply solder to the wire surface (*not* the iron surface). Since heat rises, it is best to touch the iron to the underside of the wire surface, and then touch the solder to the upper side. If the wire is hot enough, the solder will flow freely into the strands. Remove the heat, and the solder will quickly cool, effectively cementing the wire strands together, in effect creating a solid wire. Do this to all three conductors and the ground braid.

All terminal connections should be made mechanically secure before soldering. Solder is not strong, and it cannot be relied upon to hold a wire to a terminal under stress. Therefore, always loop the wire around the terminal and make sure it remains in place when you give it a small tug. Then apply the solder, heating from the underside until both surfaces are hot enough to soak up solder.

Different types of connectors require different soldering techniques. XLR connectors have hollow pins into which wires are inserted. To connect wires, heat the pin from the outside, and flow solder into the hollow pin; then insert the wire and remove the heat. The center pin of an RCA connector can be done this way also. Quarter-inch connectors usually have ring terminals, while the grounding spade may be just a flat surface. It is usually necessary to heat the connector for a while, until its temperature stabilizes, and the pin to which you are soldering becomes hot.

While soldering, if one or both of the surfaces is not hot enough, the solder may roll into a ball or bulb and simply sit on the surface, rather than spreading out over it. Although it may cover both the wire and the terminal, do not let this be your connection. It is not strong enough to remain intact, and probably is not making good electrical contact either.

Metal is a vigorous conductor of heat. If you hold the items being soldered with a large pair of metal pliers, or a massive metal vise-grip, the pliers or grip may act as a heat sink, soaking up energy from the soldering iron while the item you are intending to solder remains cool. Try to use small tools with plastic bases for supporting wires and terminals. On the other hand, if you overheat the solder, the rosin in the core of the solder will burn away. Since the rosin is a cleaning substance which enables the solder to stick to its intended surface, losing it will cause trouble. The whole process takes some practice, but by the time you're done with a full patch bay's worth of connections, you'll be an expert, I promise.

Again, I must remind you that no matter how hot solder is, it will not adhere to a cold surface. This is the nature of the dreaded "cold solder joint," a phrase you might hear as you dole out $250 in repair costs on a $300 machine. After a little jiggling during normal use, the solder connection fails, and the unit ceases to function. It takes nothing to *fix* a cold solder joint—just reheat the joint—but it can take hours to *find*.

Here are some tips on recognizing problems:

- Cold solder joints tend to be dull and bulbous, perhaps even cracked.

- Sometimes there is a "halo" or small ring around a bad connection.

A good joint will be shiny—almost mirror-like—and will conform to the shape of the surface it adheres to.

Patch Cords and Plugs

There are two different types of 1/4-inch plugs and jacks, known as *phone* and *telephone*. Phone plugs and jacks are the usual type that are found on headphones and guitar cords. They are usually made of nickel or chrome-plated steel, and have a larger diameter than the telephone plugs used in professional audio applications. The telephone plugs are commonly made of solid brass, and are the correct plugs to use in most commercial 1/4-inch patch bays. Using phone plugs may cause the patch bay contacts to be overextended, resulting in poor normal connections when the plug is removed. Of course, the telephone plugs are more expensive.

Since the patch cords are subject to constant pushing, pulling, and other types of mechanical abuse, they must be built to withstand much more than the ordinary cable assembly. Particular attention must be paid to strain relief of the wire-terminal connections. Heavy-duty patch cords can be purchased from professional audio supply stores, and may cost upwards of $20 to $30 each. It is possible to build your own patch cords using telephone plugs and high-grade cable; however, you should keep plenty of spares on hand, and be prepared to repair patch cords on a regular basis. Inserting and pulling out the patch cords by grasping the connector (not the cable) will prolong their life considerably.

Summary

The patch bay facilitates the control of signal routing in the studio. A well-designed patch bay results in more efficient use of studio time, and greater flexibility for creative use of equipment.

Proper connection techniques are important—wiring up a bay requires time and patience. There are different philosophies with regard to the design of a patch bay. Some feel that for noise control and sonic quality, patch bay wiring should be kept to a minimum. Others find the convenience of an extensive patch bay to be of great importance. Whether to have connections normalled or left open at the bay is also a matter of personal preference.

Proper soldering techniques require practice and attention to detail. Doing a good job in the construction phase will save hours of troubleshooting later.

7

ACOUSTICS

Like weather forecasting, acoustics is an inexact science at best. To the uninitiated, it more closely resembles black magic. Even today, no one really agrees on a consistent way to design a good acoustic monitoring area, and the number of different arrangements that have been tried in the name of designing a good-sounding recording space are incredible. Part of the problem is that the criteria for judging a good recording space or listening area are subjective. They involve not only sensory perceptions, but esthetic and emotional ones as well.

Another problem with the science of acoustics is that there are just too many variables. *Everything* in a studio affects the acoustic response of the room. For example, every room has its own *modal frequencies*. These are frequencies that tend to get amplified or attenuated because of the room geometry. A sound coming from the front of the room bounces off the rear wall, meets and modifies the direct source, and continues to bounce back and forth, setting up a *standing wave* at a particular frequency determined by the room dimension.

The result is that at the modal frequency, the sound pressure (loudness) near either of the walls is quite high, and is near zero towards the middle of the room. This also happens from floor to ceiling and from side to side. It gets more complicated when you begin to consider the different harmonic frequencies of the generated sound.

The entire sound field, with its up, down, front, back, left, and right modal frequencies begins to shift in time creating a weirdly moving complex pattern that can only be accurately described by an acoustic engineer using a UNIBLAB computer and 18 reams of paper. Should one decide to go through the trouble, it will largely be for naught because the entire calculation becomes meaningless when people, furniture, equipment and other irregularities are added to the room. Add to this the diversity of monitoring systems, the complex frequency contents of program material, and so on, and the whole subject could begin to remind you of some long-buried childhood nightmare.

Nevertheless, there has been considerable progress made in the field of acoustic architecture over the past few years, resulting in a glimmer of light the end of this seemingly grim tunnel. There really are things you can do to make your room sound better. I'll begin with control room acoustics.

The Monitoring Area

Before you set out to create a good monitoring area, you should understand what a good monitoring area sounds like.

In the absence of quantitative measurements, a good listening area will exhibit excellent spatial imaging and clarity. Instruments in a musical program will not sound as if they are coming from this speaker or that speaker, but rather their placement will seem to be at various points in free space. The sound field (distinctions in the stereo placement) will not vary as you move your head from side to side, and the frequency response will be relatively flat. Much of this can be perceived by a practiced listener.

Perhaps the biggest detractions from listening-area quality are early reflections (see Figure 7.1). These occur when sound bounces off surfaces close to the monitors, such as the front wall, the console surface; or the wall, floor, and ceiling surfaces between the monitors and the engineer.

Early reflections are relatively quick reflections that reach your ears a few milliseconds after the original sound, changing its characteristics. Although the ear is unable to distinguish between sounds arriving within

50 milliseconds of the direct sound, a change in the *quality* of the sound is easily perceived. This is one of the reasons that near-field monitoring has become so popular over the past few years. The proximity of the monitors to the listener reduces the amount of perceived early reflection.

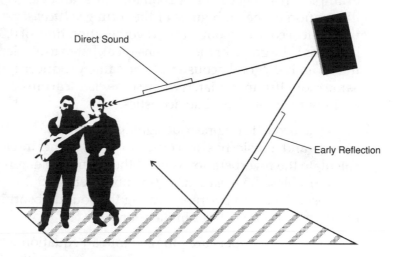

Figure 7.1 Early reflections.

You might think therefore that the ideal place to engineer a recording would be outdoors in an open field, where there are hardly any reverberations. It doesn't quite work that way. Without any reverberation (multiple reflections), the sound pressure drops off dramatically with distance from the source. This results in an unpleasant sort of acoustically "dead" feeling on the part of the listener. (If you ever get a chance to experience a true anechoic chamber, try it—it will give you the creeps.)

Reverberation Time

This brings us to an acoustic concept known as the *reverberation time* of a room. This is defined as the time it takes for all reverberant sounds in a room to die down to inaudible levels after the main sound source has stopped. There are certain reverberation times that are considered to be pretty good from an acoustic standpoint when recording or monitoring certain types of program material.

Unfortunately, reverberation times that are good for speech, for example, are not necessarily good for music and vice versa. This is a good illustration of the ambiguity of the term *good acoustics*. A producer may walk into a control room with a reverberation time of 0.35 seconds (which happens to be great for the spoken voice), listen to a voice program and say the room has "good acoustics." The same producer might walk into the same room 10 minutes later, when some classical music is being monitored and say the room has "bad acoustics."

The acoustic engineer designing a room that will be handling both speech and music has to come up with some in-between figure. To calculate the reverberation time of the room, the engineer must consider two variables: the *room volume* (in cubic feet), and the *collective absorption coefficient*—the number representing the sound-absorbing characteristics of all the various surfaces in the room.

The two numbers are plugged into an equation which gives you the theoretical reverberation time of the room. In actuality, this is a very, very rough guess—because it does not take into account the effect of people and equipment in the room, nor does it easily account for the effects of irregular room geometries. Since it's usually difficult to alter the volume of the room, the engineer will specify different surfaces to be used in the construction, which will bring the calculation closer to the desired value.

If you're interested in actually going through this exercise, there are several books available on acoustic theory that will explain the subject to you engineering masochists in much better detail. I have listed some of them in Appendix A.

Diffusion

You must allow for some reverberation, but reverberation can be detrimental to the program material. Catch-22? Not completely. Reverberation from relatively uniform surfaces produces a reflected waveform similar in time and frequency characteristics to the original. This is what causes most of the problem. If we treat the rear wall surfaces with structures known as *phase grating diffusers*, the resulting reflections are scattered about in time (see Figure 7.2).

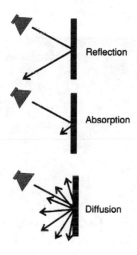

Figure 7.2   Three types of sound reflection.

There are several designs of diffusers available commercially. Figures 7.3 and 7.4 show two of them. This diffusion of reflected sound results in a dense, nonuniform array of reverberation that the human ear perceives as a pleasant ambiance. It also tends to break up standing waves, cutting down on relative peaks and valleys in the listening spectrum.

Live End Dead End Design

In an ideal monitoring situation, you would hear diffuse reverberation without early reflection. This idea has been captured and implemented in a system called *LEDE* or *Live End Dead End* control room design. *Note:* the term Live End Dead End, LEDE, is proprietary as applied to acoustics. You cannot advertise yourself as an LEDE facility unless your room is verified to meet certain rigorous criteria set by the inventors of the concept. Meeting these criteria could be expensive for a project studio budget; you can, however, design your control room with these concepts in mind.

Figure 7.3   RPG Omniffusor.

Figure 7.4 ART Diffusor.

Begin by looking at the paths that sound will take on its journey from the monitor speakers to the listening area. If the monitors (other than near-field types) are flush-mounted in the forward wall, forward wall reflections are minimized (see Figure 7.5). If not, the resulting early reflections from behind the speakers tend to complicate things.

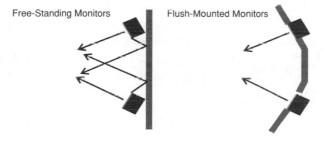

Figure 7.5 Flush-mounted vs. free-standing monitors.

The Reflection-Free Zone

The LEDE design centers around the concept of a Reflection-Free Zone, or (surprise) RFZ, otherwise known to the acoustically hip as the *sweet spot*. No area in the room is completely free of reflection, but in the Reflection-Free Zone, the listener will be reasonably free of early reflections—meaning that the sound heard is the directly emanated monitor speaker sound, followed by diffused late reflections from the back wall. Figure 7.6 is a graphic representation of the RFZ in a control room. The lines represent the directions of sound through the room, and show various reflection angles.

The smallest room dimension limits the size of the RFZ that can be created. Lately, there have been geometric treatments introduced into some control rooms that will extend the sweet spot back past the engineer's area to the producer's desk. Normally this would require a raised ceiling; however, it is possible to divert most early reflections by applying acoustic absorbers to wedge-shaped walls and ceilings (see Figure 7.7).

The front wall of an LEDE room is usually covered with acoustically absorbent material, such as an acoustic wedge foam. Often, the floor in front of the console, and perhaps the side of the console that faces the monitors, are covered with absorbent material, as shown in Figure 7.8. The primary limitation of acoustic absorbers is that few (if any) single types of acoustic treatment can absorb all frequencies. Most popular commercial acoustic-foam wall coverings (such as Sonex) have a reduced effect on frequencies under 500Hz. Absorption of lower audible frequencies using porous materials or foam can only be achieved using porous material with a thickness comparable to the wavelength of the sound. At 100 Hz, the wavelength is 11.3 feet, so you can see that this approach would not be practical.

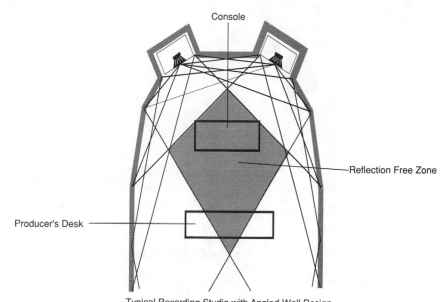

Typical Recording Studio with Angled Wall Design
(Courtesy of Bill Morrison, Acoustical Physics Laboratories)

Figure 7.6   RFZ reflections.

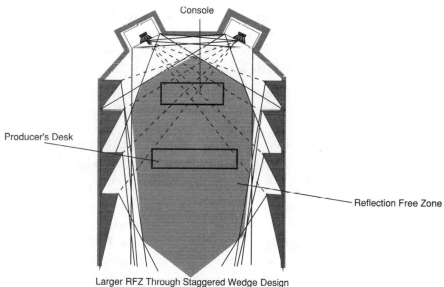

Larger RFZ Through Staggered Wedge Design
(Courtesy of Bill Morrison, Acoustical Physics Laboratories)

Figure 7.7   Using a wedge design for a larger RFZ.

139

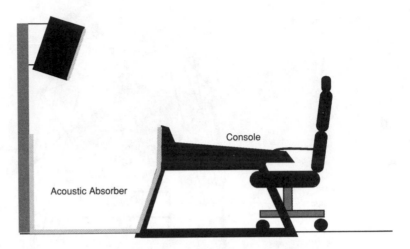

Figure 7.8 Absorbent material applied to the front of the console.

As an alternative, there are *resonant absorbers* or *bass traps* that can be introduced to counteract a possible boominess in the bass frequencies. Bass traps or resonators usually involve some kind of tuned air cavity. They are typically constructed of a barrier material, followed by an air space, and then another barrier. A typical stud-and-sheetrock wall, built a few feet out from a foundation (instead of directly against it), is an excellent bass trap. There is often not enough room at the forward wall for the bass trap, so it can be located or constructed as part of the back wall.

If the monitor speakers are flush mounted, it's possible to keep the forward wall live, yet still achieve a Reflection-Free Zone at the listening area. This is done by diverting the reflections away from the engineer's listening area by angling the walls and ceilings; the control room shown in Figure 7.6 is a typical example of this design. If the walls and ceilings are already in place, you can install angled acoustic panels on these surfaces.

Be careful, though. You cannot arbitrarily angle the walls and expect to achieve good results. The exact angles must be computed using acoustic modeling techniques that are beyond the scope of this book and possibly beyond the scope of the average project studio design budget.

As a possible alternative to much of this hair pulling, RPG Diffusor Systems now markets what they call a "studio in a box." It is a complete set of panel absorber/diffusors for the side and rear walls of a control room, designed to provide a reasonably good listening area in nearly any room. The cost for the set is $1200. For $1650, additional ceiling panels can be included.

Equalization?

After carefully designing the control room to achieve absolute sonic excellence, everything you add to the room—mixing console, tape machines, chairs, tables, even speakers—becomes an acoustic detriment. Not only does sound bounce off these things and get back to you, but they also *resonate*, sending out new vibrations at various sympathetic frequencies. Untreated, these resonances and reverberations color the sounds from your monitors, and turn the frequency response curve of your listening area (which you foolishly hoped would be flat) into a gnarled, twisted, serpentine affair.

Some people try to remedy these problems by throwing an equalizer on the monitor outputs to boost and cut frequencies in the program material, which (supposedly) counteracts the room acoustics at the listening area. This doesn't really work, because it doesn't correct the *time-arrival misinformation* caused by the reflections. Time-arrival misinformation not only affects the frequency of the signal, but also affects the perception of where the sound sources originate. The result is that the stereo field is distorted.

The room is the culprit, therefore it is the room that must be treated. You can do this by trying to find out which frequencies are being affected by objects and surfaces in the room. Then, by trial and error, you dampen these frequencies—using acoustic treatment, absorbers, diffusers, and all the other methods that are probably familiar by now. (There are measuring techniques that can help you in these efforts; the equipment is quite sophisticated, however, and it requires a knowledgeable operator.)

Measurements

Earlier I referred to the frequency-response curve of the room, which implies that measurements can be taken to determine the shape of this curve for a given room. In fact, there are a number of measurements of acoustic response that can be done, mostly with the aid of expensive Time-Delay Spectrometry (TDS) equipment. These measurements, sometimes referred to as Time-Energy-Frequency (or, you guessed it, TEF) measurements, are best handled by qualified consultants. To the untrained, the resulting curves generated by TDS equipment may be meaningless. If you want to give it a try, however, there are several professional audio houses that rent this type of equipment on a daily basis.

The Recording Area

In the recording area, it is not necessary to achieve a Reflection-Free Zone; however, most of the monitor-area concepts apply here as well. A completely dead acoustic space results in flat-sounding musical instruments. On the other hand, exaggerated modal frequencies may produce boominess or overly pronounced discolorations in the recorded sound. Some of these can be reduced by applying acoustic absorber material to the wall surfaces, as shown in Figure 7.9.

Figure 7.9 The drum area with acoustic treatment.

Diffusion is also helpful here. Once your equipment has been installed, try recording different instruments in the studio talent area and see if you can determine where there might be reverberation problems. This is further discussed in Chapter 9.

It's conceivable that, because of the room dimensions, it may be impossible to counteract the negative acoustic effects of the room. In this case the remedy might be to make the room acoustically dead using acoustic absorbers and traps; then use a digital signal processor to add ambient reverb and other processing during the recording process to bring the sound back to life.

Your Ears Are the Judge

On the type of budget that most project studios are built, it may be difficult to implement a sophisticated, carefully engineered acoustic design. In that case, you've got to trust your ears. After installing the equipment into the room, try to judge the clarity and stereo separation of different types of program material. Also, since your ears might not be perfect, enlist some of your friends who listen to music often, and try to get a consensus.

A good idea is to use familiar CDs of different types of music. Listen at varying volume levels, and see if you can discern major frequency boosts or cuts as you raise volume from moderate listening levels to fairly loud levels. Move things around in the room (where possible) and note the effects.

Record some music mixes and take them to other places to listen to them. Is there a consistent lack of bass in your mixes? Are the highs too high? These are indications of peaks or crevices in your room's frequency response curves. Try adding absorbers in certain areas. You may be able to pinpoint areas where absorbers can help by positioning a heavy blanket in various places and listening to the effect on the program material.

Summary

There are many factors that contribute to the overall sound of a recording or listening area. Much has to do with room dimensions, and as mentioned in Chapter 1, going out of your way to redimension a room will most likely be pointless if the overall volume of the room is less than 1500 cubic feet.

The most important characteristics of a good monitoring area are good spatial imaging and clarity of sound. Complicated program material should not sound muddled or indistinct. A good recording area will enhance the quality of instruments or speech without sounding "dead," and again will not cause any frequencies to sound slurred or muddy.

Table 7.1 shows the different room characteristics that can be considered and the factors that contribute to them.

Table 7.1 Acoustic effects and their causes

Room Characteristic	*Caused by*
Modal frequencies	Room dimensions
Reverberation time	Room volume and surface treatments
Early reflections	Proximity of speakers to listener
	Room geometry
	Surface treatments
Diffusion	Surface treatments

Most of these phenomena can be measured using sophisticated measuring equipment. On a limited budget, trust your ears and the ears of a friend. Try moving surfaces or objects in the room and judiciously applying acoustic absorbers or reflectors.

8

CONSTRUCTION: FINISHING TOUCHES

Once all the heavy work is done—sheetrock installed, spackled, and caulked, windows and doors mounted, wiring led out, and so on—it's time to do the completion work.

Preparation

Painting all the walls before the carpets and moldings are installed will save quite a bit of time that would otherwise be spent covering them with dropcloths and masking tape. Before turning on and using the electrical outlets, make sure all connections have been cleaned and tightened, and cover plates have been installed.

Dust is one of a studio's worst enemies (next to cigarette smoke), and it will continue to settle in the room for several days after spackling and sanding the walls and ceilings. Before beginning your finishing work, try to remove as much dust as humanly possible. Vacuum frequently, and wipe the walls and ceilings down with rags dampened in mineral spirits. After vacuuming, damp mop the unfinished floors. If you aren't fanatical about zapping dust now, it will come back to haunt you later.

Carpet and/or flooring is the final touch, and you will find that the room suddenly seems finished once the floors are completed.

Equipment Racks and Stands

Audio equipment manufacturers don't seem to be willing to agree on much in the way of standardizing things. However, they have been able to agree on one standard, and that is the standard for rack-mount equipment dimensions. Nearly all outboard equipment, tape decks, line conditioners, patch bay panels, power amplifiers and test devices manufactured today fit into a standard rack space or some multiple of rack spaces.

The exact dimensions of a single rack space are 19 1/4 inches wide by 1 1/4 inches high. Equipment size is often specified in terms of rack spaces; for example, an EMU Proteus sound generator takes up one rack space, while an Akai S950 Sampler takes up two rack spaces. A dbx de-esser uses half a rack space, which means that two such devices can be placed side by side in a single rack space, with the proper mounting hardware.

Special Grounding Considerations

Remember that ground hum occurs when a ground loop is present—meaning that a path other than the main path to ground is available to the equipment. The grounding pin of the electrical cord on most audio equipment is electrically connected to the metal enclosure of the equipment. If that enclosure is then screwed into a metal rack (as shown in Figure 8.1), the rack now provides an electrical connection to the next piece of equipment mounted to it—instant ground loop. There are two ways around this, and you should keep them in mind when installing equipment into any type of rack.

The first (and most common) method is to defeat the power cord ground connection of all the units mounted to the rack. Then bond each piece of equipment to the structure of the rack, using a dedicated copper wire running from the enclosure to the rack itself. (This ensures a better connection than just the equipment enclosure resting against the rack.) Next, run a #10 AWG copper wire from the rack to the main system ground–this wire will serve as the only path to ground for all the rack mounted units.

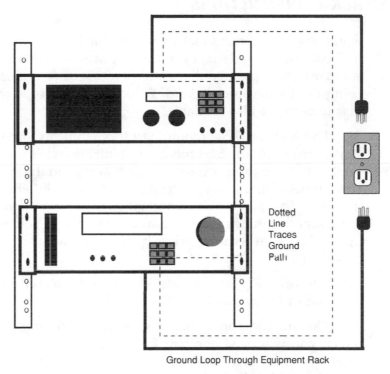

Dotted
Line
Traces
Ground
Path

Ground Loop Through Equipment Rack

Figure 8.1   A Ground Loop Through Equipment Rack

The second (and less effective) method is to retain the original equipment grounds, making sure that all the equipment is plugged into the same circuit. Then, electrically isolate the enclosures from the rack by inserting nonmetallic spacers between the equipment flanges and the rack. Use plastic screws to secure the equipment to the rack. One problem with this approach is that each device may still contact the device mounted above or below it, simply because it fits tightly into the rack.

Rack Constructions

Stand alone equipment racks are available from all audio supply stores; they come in myriad shapes and sizes, but all are configured to mount the standard rack space equipment. There are several designs, one choice being the tubular metal stand. Wooden cabinet-type racks and tubular plastic racks are also available.

The cost for these mounting racks is, in my opinion, rather high, considering that suitable units can be built into walls or constructed by the do it yourselfer for much less. The advantage to the store bought stand-alone units is that many of them are mounted on wheels and are easily movable. This may be an important consideration if you use the studio space for other things when you are not recording. You may be able to pick up used racks at reduced prices by checking with surplus companies or classified ads.

The following are some ideas for creating custom racks to suit the size and shape of your studio.

The one component item common to all designs is the *rack rail*, of which you will need one pair for every rack you build. Rack rails are available in standard and custom lengths, and are nothing more than angled metal brackets with tapped screw holes set at the intervals shown in Figure 8.2. When ordering, specify the number of rack spaces the rails should accommodate. The approximate cost for a pair of 10-inch-spaced rack rails is $15.00.

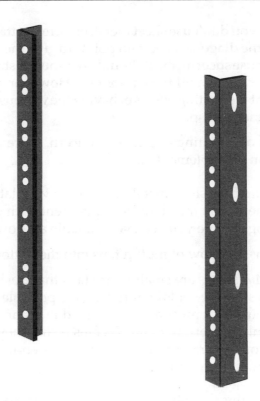

Figure 8.2 Rack rails.

The following are two types of rack construction that can be used in place of store bought racks.

Metal Cage Construction

Although this is not the most glamorous approach, it will work fine if you're on a tight budget. Slotted metal angle brackets can be obtained at any hardware store. These can be bolted together to form a cubic structure to which a pair of rack rails can be mounted at the front face. Sheet metal can be screwed to the sides and rear of the equipment racks to hide wiring and give a more finished look. If properly grounded, the sheet metal may also act as a shield against electromagnetic noise.

If you don't use sheet metal, be sure to attach metal reinforcing strips along the diagonal at certain points to give the structure some strength. If you do use sheet metal, it should give you the structural strength necessary for the rack to hold the equipment. However, you may need to take into account the heating effects of having the various devices mounted together in an enclosed space.

If overheating becomes a concern, there are two possible remedies that can be implemented:

- Purchase sheet metal panels with ventilation openings cut into them. You may have to experiment with placement of the openings before you achieve a suitable air flow.

- Install a row of muffin fans into the bottom of the rack.

  Muffin fans are small rotary fans that push air up through the rack system for cooling purposes. It's possible to purchase a bank of four to six muffin fans mounted in a standard rack space tray. The only concern with muffin fans is that they are noisy. The noise from several fans may be obtrusive enough to interfere with monitoring or recording.

Ideally, the cube you build to house your equipment should be at least 30 inches deep, to accommodate the various types of equipment and wiring you might run across. Remember that connectors plugged into the back of a rack mount device add two to three inches to the depth required.

If your space is really tight, you can buy 90-degree angle connectors. These are available for both 1/4-inch and XLR connections, and will buy you about an inch of clearance over the straight type.

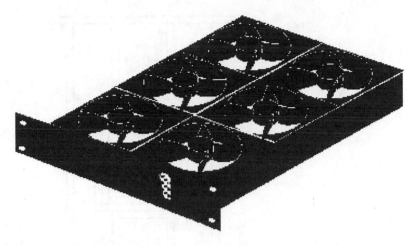

Figure 8.3 Installing muffin fans in a rack.

Wall Mount Racks

The second approach is to mount equipment directly into a wall. If you find this approach practical for your studio, you need to do three things:

- Be sure there is enough clearance behind the wall to install the equipment and associated connectors. (Also provide additional clearance above and below the equipment, to allow for adequate heat dissipation.)

- Provide access to the rear of the units for wiring changes, maintenance and repair. You can either provide an entry into the area behind the wall or, by mounting the entire setup on a hinge, provide swing out access to the units. This latter method is not recommended for the inexperienced builder, as it is difficult to build a hinged structure that has the proper strength and wire clearance capabilities.

- Build a suitable two-by-four frame into the existing stud construction to which the rack rails will be mounted (see Figure 8.4).

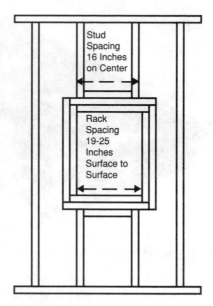

Figure 8.4 Framing for rack rails.

It is usually possible to mount the rack rails so that they will rest far enough out from the surface of the stud to allow the equipment to sit flush with the sheetrock wall surface. The outer wall can then be finished using one-inch wood moulding.

Empty Spaces

Naturally, if you mount five pieces of single-rack-space equipment into an eight-space rack, you're going to end up with three empty spaces in the rack. What's behind a rack is rarely aesthetically pleasing—in fact it's usually a mess of wire backed by an unpainted cabinet cover. So you'll probably want to mask those empty spaces with blank panels. Of course, when your equipment upgrade dreams come true, you can replace all the blank panels with marvelously impressive new devices.

The problem I ran across is that the blank metal panels that were available through audio dealers seemed strangely expensive—roughly $12 to $17 for a two space panel. Is a small, flat piece of metal really worth $17? Since I had deliberately put in much more rack space than I needed at the time, I had a lot of spaces to fill. I found myself deliberating whether to order $170 worth of blank panels (10 panels at $17), and I didn't relish the prospect.

Instead, I drew out the dimensions of a single blank rack space, indicated the size and shape of the four screw holes, brought the drawing to a local machine shop, and asked how much it would cost to crank out about twenty of these babies in 1/8-inch-thick brushed aluminum. It turned out to be less than $170. I was able to have twenty panels made for under $100, resulting in a net cost of about $5 per panel.

There's no guarantee that your local machine shop will be as inexpensive as mine, but if you need a lot of blanks, try showing them a copy of Figure 8.5 and getting a price on the quantity you need. If there's a sheet metal shop in your vicinity, they will probably do it even cheaper than a machine shop. Often the price per piece goes way down as you order more pieces, so ask your musician friends if they need any, and place the orders together.

As an alternative to metal blanks, try plain fiberboard–painted flat black—as an interim solution. Carefully sanded and painted, it looks good and costs very little.

Instead of blanks, some companies are now offering useful and innovative rack space fillers. There are shelves designed to be rack mounted that will hold cassettes, CDs, or DAT tapes. There are lockable cabinet-type units, slide out drawers and numerous other feature laden products. All of these are, of course, more expensive than blank panels, but their efficient use of otherwise-useless space may be worth it.

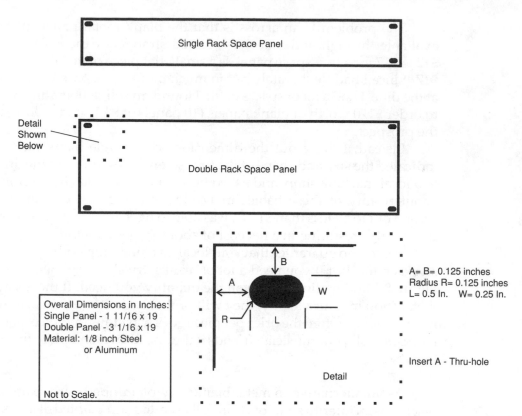

Figure 8.5 A blank rack panel.

Equipment Cabinets

In Studio B, plans called for an equipment cabinet/keyboard table to be built and located behind the engineer's seat at the console. This allows the engineer to access equipment controls from the chair, and also allows keyboard players to hear the monitors from the "sweet spot."

The cabinet would be constructed of wood, with a Formica top. The cabinet was designed to be wide enough for three standard 19-inch equipment racks to be mounted in the front face, and for a keyboard controller and a computer to sit comfortably on top. At least four inches were left between each mounting rack to allow for structural bracing.

The front face was angled slightly to make viewing and manual access to the outboard equipment easier for the engineers. The table height had to be suitable for a keyboard player to sit and play comfortably. I measured the key height on a standard piano and calculated the height needed for the table surface, knowing that the keys on an electronic keyboard would sit approximately four inches above it.

Figure 8.6 shows a diagram of the cabinet. I decided that one side of the cabinet would be left open, and that this side would be located flush with the side wall of the studio. Audio and electrical wiring (which was led from the patch bay through the studio wall) could be routed directly into the cabinet.

The cabinet face opposite the equipment racks was provided with hinged doors for access to the equipment wiring and connections. I had no experience with designing furniture, but with this diagram and a clear idea of what I wanted, it wasn't difficult to convey the cabinet requirements to a cabinet builder.

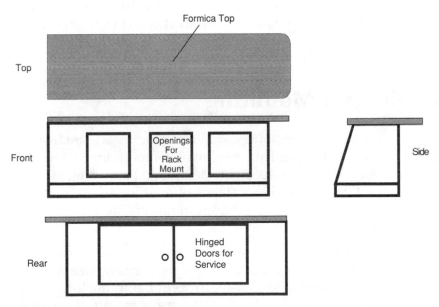

Figure 8.6 The layout for the cabinet.

The cabinet maker was astute enough to ask a few questions, and I'm glad he did. He wanted to know how heavy the equipment was that would be mounted into the cabinet, and what kind of load the Formica top was expected to bear.

I checked the manufacturer's specs on the various devices that would be mounted into the cabinet and came up with an average weight per rack space that was used for design purposes. To support the equipment, the front face and the corner bracings needed to be reinforced a little stronger than would be standard for a typical household furniture cabinet.

The cabinet was custom-built of high grade pine, and finished in a stain that matched the color of the wood floor in the studio. The Formica top was matched to the grey color scheme of the walls, carpet and upholstery. Cost for the cabinet was less than $1000, and the resulting piece is extremely functional and good-looking.

One possible drawback to a dedicated cabinet such as this one is that it may have little resale value if you need to expand or reconfigure your studio. It is worth balancing this concern against the cost of three store bought rack stands (roughly $150 each) and a commercial keyboard/ computer stand (roughly $250). It costs only $300 more for a high-grade piece of furniture that is capable of much more than the commercial stands. (You can see the finished product back in Chapter 1, Figure 1.9.)

Monitor Mounting

For near field monitors, standard practice is to mount them directly to the console bridge. This may involve modifying or tapping into the bridge itself. If you're reluctant to do this, you may prefer to mount the monitors on floor stands. Floor stands offer at least two advantages: they may be more movable than a bridge mounting, and there will be no vibrational coupling with the console.

Bridge mounting can be accomplished in several ways. Usually, a small platform about the size of the speaker base is built of wood or metal and fastened to the console. Before attempting to mount the monitors, you may want to consult with the console manufacturer, who might know of a good way to do it. Obviously, you don't want to screw anything into the console bridge without first determining what lies beyond the sheet metal.

Sending a metal screw or bolt into an area where live electrical components reside is not only potentially damaging to the console, but might cause the entire enclosure to become electrically live and not particularly friendly to the people who might touch it.

One method of fastening that does not involve drilling or tapping into the console is to use a vice or C clamp as shown in Figure 8.7. General-use C clamps can be purchased through hardware supply stores or catalogs.

For wall mount or soffit mount monitors (a *soffit* is a horizontal shelf built into the wall or ceiling), the main goal is to isolate the monitors acoustically from the wall structure. If the monitor is mounted directly to the wall, or if it sits directly on the soffit structure, sound vibrations will be transmitted from the speaker cabinets through the wall—resulting in a loss of soundproofing integrity, and/or an enhancement of undesirable acoustic resonancing.

Usually soffit-mounted monitors are surrounded by layers of *rock wool*, which is a type of acoustic insulation that dampens the vibration from the speaker cabinets. Before enclosing studio monitors into a soffit, contact the monitor manufacturer. You'll want to determine whether there might be any problems with monitor performance if they are boxed into a wall structure. The manufacturer may specify minimum dimensions for the soffit cavity to ensure proper system performance.

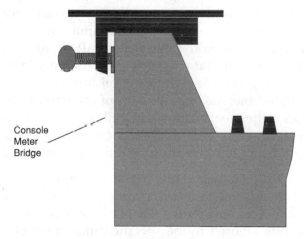

Console
Meter
Bridge

Figure 8.7 A C clamp.

Mounting monitors to the wall or ceiling using a screw-in type bracket is the least desirable situation; however, if you are forced to do so, put some resilient material like rubber or foam between the bracket face and the wall or ceiling. Another possibility is to hang the monitors, using cable or chain led down from the ceiling. In that situation, it is important to fasten the cable or chain securely to the strongest possible ceiling frame member—and to fasten the cable or chain adequately to the monitor itself. Monitors are heavy, and are constantly vibrating. Make it a point to check the fasteners every week or so—you wouldn't want them to fall and cause damage or injury.

Microphone Mounting

The high-quality microphones used for vocals and other applications in the studio tend to be quite sensitive; they can pick up stray vibrations very easily—especially through the mike stand or mounting mechanism.

In my isolation booth, for example, I thought it would be clever to mount the vocal mike to a hinged arm bolted to the wall, rather than take up precious floor space with a mike stand. Unfortunately, simply bolting a store bought, spring-loaded, hinged arm mechanism to the isolation booth wall—and then mounting a supersensitive condenser mike to it— caused more grief than you can imagine. Every time someone walked *anywhere* in the house, the structural vibrations set up a standing wave in the metal arm that was picked up by the microphone as a kind of earth-shattering rumble. When the oil burner kicked on in the next room, it sounded like the engine room of the battleship *Missouri*. If the vocalists tapped their feet on the floor while singing, a whole new rhythm track was created, and if they hit the right note, the springs in the arm mechanism would sing out like some kind of weird metallic choir.

Rule Number One: avoid mounting microphones to the dwelling frame. Also, if you use a mike stand and you still pick up unwanted vibrations, consider the use of a shock-mount microphone holder. Shock mounts tailored to the specific dimensions of the more popular micro-phones are available from audio dealers. Ranging in price from $35 to $150, these elaborate shock-absorbing mechanisms consist of rubber or metal springs that don't make noise. They enable the microphone to "float" in a vibration-free manner.

Security Systems

Protect your investment—install a good security system. You can go crazy barring windows and bolting doors, but if burglars want to get in, they will. True, a determined intruder may just keep going and ignore your alarm siren or bell, but that's not likely—especially if the intention is to unobtrusively make off with big bulky equipment like consoles or multi-track tape decks.

For good security, you need a good system. You don't have to spend a fortune, but the basic "plug it into the wall and it works" type of security devices are not good security; they can usually be defeated by a criminal with half a brain and a survival instinct. You need to design and install a system that is tailored to work effectively in your studio, does not trip every time the cat burps, and is not easily defeatable. If you do it yourself, you can probably design and install a good system that will not only protect the studio, but also the rest of your house for about $400.

Having just completed the design and construction of a rather complicated audio production facility, you should have little trouble designing and installing an alarm system. The following is basic information intended to steer you toward a quality installation. I suggest you obtain further information before actually purchasing or installing your system. I have listed some good "do it yourself" alarm system books in the bibliography.

The basic security system consists of a control panel, a sound source and sensors. The design process is largely a matter of being crafty—make like you are the burglar deviously attempting to break into the studio.

Sensors

There are various types of sensing devices that can be used together as part of a security system:

- space protection sensors
- weight detection sensors
- glass breakage detectors

- smoke/heat detectors
- water detectors

When designing the system, look at all the possible access paths to the studio. Obviously the doors and windows should be fitted with sensors that can detect their opening. However, there may be other ways into the building (through upper-story windows, side hallways, and so on). It may be necessary to design what are known as *interior traps*. These consist of motion detectors covering a certain area, pressure pads placed under carpeting on stairs or in high-traffic areas, and simple switches under equipment that is likely to be taken that will trip the alarm if the equipment is moved.

Control Panels

The control panel is the heart and brains of the system. Usually, installing the panel is simply a matter of attaching it to the wall, connecting it to power and then connecting all the sensor wires to a terminal block inside the panel. Some features that are available on control panels include delay circuits, instant circuits, a panic-switch connection, and remote keypad connections.

Audible and Inaudible Alarms

There are a few different types of alarm sound generators available. Most popular are the siren and the bell.

As another alternative, you can have your alarm system connected to a service agency that will notify you at a given number if your alarm is tripped. You can choose to have a silent alarm in your studio, or to have an audible siren or bell in addition to the central station notification. There is usually a monthly fee associated with the alarm service agency.

Acoustic Foam

If you've read Chapter 7, you probably have an idea of where you want to apply acoustic foam tiles. Fortunately, they're easy to put up; however, they're nearly impossible to get down without making a mess of both the walls and the foam.

Most acoustic foam manufacturers specify various types of adhesives that can be used to mount the tiles. Actually, almost any hardware store can supply a tube of household tile or carpet adhesive that can be applied to the foam or the wall using a caulking gun and work just fine. These adhesives are permanent, so you should decide exactly where you want this stuff to go and how it should be positioned before you glue it.

One studio I know of used Velcro to apply the foam tiles to the wall, and as such, could move and reposition the tiles whenever it was appropriate. Seems like an interesting idea to me.

Chairs and Other Furniture

The importance of a good chair (or set of chairs) for the recording engineer cannot be overemphasized. Recording sessions sometimes last many hours, and fatigue will set in early if you are uncomfortably seated. This not only puts a cramp in the creativity process, but it may affect the quality of your work to a noticeable degree—something you don't want to find yourself explaining to a client.

Here are some features to look for in a good chair:

- The back should be straight at shoulder level and slightly convex at where it touches the spine.

- The small of your back should fit snugly into the chair back.

- Cushions should be relatively firm–soft cushions roll up around your joints and put pressure on them.

- Arm supports should be firm, padded, and at least two inches wide.

- Height should be adjustable, as well as tilt.

Pick a chair that is mobile (rolls easily) and has plenty of support. There are newer chairs, ergonomically designed to accommodate the computer workstations of the world, that claim to increase productivity by a fair percentage. I don't know how true the claims are, but many of the "ergonomically correct" chairs I sampled were extremely comfortable.

Also a big help for those endless sessions is a couch where groupies, idle musicians and other potential nuisance persons can slump into and be useless without being bothersome. Many larger studios have a separate lounge for hanging out (some even have workout rooms, food services, overnight lodging, and swimming pools, but that's a different league). If you have some spare room, you might want to consider making a separate lounge area—it's the kind of touch that might draw clients.

Summary

The finishing touches are just as important as the basic construction. For a truly professional look, finish all rough edges with molding and trim. Install all equipment into neat, functional equipment racks, and create a comfortable, effective environment for recording. Use quality furniture, especially the chairs for the recording engineers and producers.

To protect your investment, secure all possible entrances with good window and door locks, and install an alarm system specifically designed for the layout of your studio.

9

THE FUN STUFF: INSTALLATION AND TROUBLESHOOTING

Probably the most exciting day for me (after months of intense planning and hard work) was the day the delivery truck carrying about 80 percent of the studio equipment pulled up into my driveway. It took three men to carry the console down the stairs to the basement that had been carefully constructed and wired to accept it. The unit was positioned on its stand, the cover was removed and it seemed as if the room was transformed from a basement into a recording studio at that moment.

As we unpacked boxes containing signal processors, amplifiers, sound generators and tape machines, my friends and I began to talk about the projects that would be undertaken in our new facility. What I had dreamed about since getting my first glimpse of a recording studio 15 years earlier had finally come to pass. I guess the realization crept up on me slowly, and then hit me full force. It felt good.

Throughout the process of all the design, budgeting, construction, wiring, and finishing work there are many times when I found myself thinking, "I must be crazy. Is it worth all this effort?" Once the equipment arrived and began to make sounds (good or bad), the question never came up again.

Unpacking

Whether you purchase your equipment in bulk or acquire it piece by piece, there are some prudent steps you should take upon receiving any unit. If you do buy in bulk, deal with one unit at a time to avoid confusion later. Unpacking several boxes at once is an invitation to scatter small accessories around, lose items, mix up packing material that should be saved for later use, and so on.

From the time a device is tested at the factory to the time it arrives at your studio, a lot can happen to it. It may have been flown several thousand miles and then trucked a few hundred more before reaching the dealer, and the journey is not always pleasant.

I once brought a delicate package back from Japan, so to protect it, I had the packer stamp "FRAGILE" in huge letters all over the box. Later, at the airport in New York, I watched as a baggage handler picked it up and threw it twenty feet across the room onto a conveyor which proceeded to dump suitcase after suitcase on top of it.

You probably wouldn't conceive of taking one of your new machines in its box and throwing it across the room to hit the wall and fall to the floor, but this is the kind of thing that it has probably been subjected to many times already. Aside from the physical abuse, it may have been exposed to temperature extremes that would kill most carbon based organisms.

Most manufacturers will include a concise list of what is packaged with the unit somewhere in the paperwork. This is the first thing you want to find. If you are picking up your equipment at the dealer, check each and every box for manuals, warranty papers, power cords, connectors, remote control units, battery packs, transformers, disks, foot pedals, and every other accessory that could possibly belong with the product.

If anything is missing, pack up the unit and ask for a new one; then start the process over with that one. If the dealer does not have another unit (or the missing item), do not leave the store with the device, and do not pay for it. Sometimes without the incentive for a sale, the dealer will take forever to replace the part. If the dealer offers to replace the item with a part from a demo unit, ask him to reduce the price accordingly, and then only after checking out the item to be sure it is functional.

If the equipment is being delivered, you won't be able to remedy the missing item problem on the spot, but be sure to carefully document what is missing and report it to the dealer immediately.

Testing the Equipment

Before installing the equipment in its final location and connecting it through the studio wiring to the patch bay or the console, connect each piece of audio gear directly to inputs and outputs that you know are functioning. Make sure the audio cables and connectors you are using are in perfect working condition.

When testing a reverb unit (for example), if you don't get an output or an indication of an input signal from the device, you want to eliminate the possibility that something in the wiring chain is not functioning (or not patched correctly). This way, you isolate the problem to the Equipment Under Test. (At the risk of sounding like the kind of guy who takes a calculator to bed with him, I'm going to refer to the device from this point on as the EUT.)

If you receive a large delivery of many pieces, set up a small test bench near an electrical outlet, with access to a sound source (keyboard or other signal generator) and a monitor system (amplifier/speaker combination), and check the operation of each piece. Before making a judgement as to whether the EUT is working properly or not, make sure you understand the operation of the unit and the function of all the major controls. Always have the operator's manual on hand for the checkout procedure, and pay particular attention to the connection configurations and start-up recommendations.

Many of us have been using equipment of this nature for years, and it's easy to get cocky. Unless you're very familiar with the particular model you're checking out, don't assume that you know how to work it. Design engineers have a knack for coming up with incomprehensible and deviously subtle changes to operating procedures for new models of equipment.

Also, try to check out every function or operating mode (within reason) before satisfying yourself that the EUT is A-OK. You'll be disappointed if you try to use the automatic punch-in feature on your multitrack for the first time one month after the warranty runs out—and you find that the feature doesn't work. This will also save you the embarrassment of finding out during a paid session.

Checkout Procedures

Here are some helpful checkout procedures for most equipment types:

For All Equipment

1. Connect all audio input and output cables, remote-control cables, MIDI connections, and so on, and verify that everything is routed correctly.

2. Make sure the power switch is off and plug in the equipment.

3. Turn volume knobs down on both the EUT and other connected equipment, and then power up the EUT.

Most devices will indicate whether the unit is on, either by lights, character displays, audible beeps, or some similar method. If the unit obviously did not turn on, check the owner's manual again and make sure that what you did was supposed to make it go on. If you're still nowhere, unplug the EUT, and see if there is a fuse at the input of the device.

Input fuses are usually located near the point where the power cord enters the machine. You can generally tell if a fuse is blown by looking at it. A good fuse will have a silver wire running intact from one end of the fuse to the other. If the wire is ruptured or if there is discoloration of the glass, replace it with the same type and rating of fuse. Then recheck the connections to the device before turning the unit on.

Improper connection is a major cause of blown fuses. If the connections are correct, it's possible that a line surge or some other transient problem caused the fuse to open, and the unit will now function properly.

Unfortunately, it's more probable that the problem that caused the fuse to open is internal and still present in the machine. This means the fuse may blow again as soon as you turn on the device. If this happens, return the unit to the dealer.

Analog Tape Decks

1. Most tape decks should be given a few minutes to warm up after turning on the power. Clean the heads, load tape (I recommend a suspendable tape), and then put the deck in record mode and feed signals to all inputs, one at a time. Be sure the signal is at the proper level for the tape deck input, and always apply the signal gradually, increasing its level slowly until you reach 0db in the deck's input VU meter(s).

2. Adjust the level of the input signal up and down and check the response of VU meters. It's probably not a good idea to try to calibrate the input meters at this time. Save all calibration work for the time when the deck is installed in its final resting place, and all permanent audio connections are functioning.

3. Record some clear, steady tones to tape on each channel at 0db. If you have a signal generator, use a 1Khz sine wave. If not, try using a flute sound from a synthesizer at around middle C. Play back the tones and check for output. Keep an ear open for severe signal degradation or marked wavering on playback of a steady tone. Keep in mind that all tape decks will degrade signal somewhat, especially if they are out of calibration. Don't worry about minute differences in sound just yet.

4. If the tape machine has built-in noise reduction, try recording and playing back tones with NR switched in and out. If you have some prerecorded material in that format, try playing it back, watching for unusual signal levels or lack of frequency response at the high or low end.

5. Try all transport functions–fast forward, rewind, search functions, speed variations, automatic punch in/punch out, spool, and so on. For open reel machines, keep an eye on how well the tape spools

from one reel to the other under all speed conditions. The tape should wind smoothly and quietly onto the opposite reel with a minimum of protruding edges on the wound side. If the tape rubs against the reel edges, make sure that the tape hubs are tight and the reels are not warped. Moderately poor spooling may only require a braking adjustment. However, lots of noise from the spools or severe misspooling could indicate transport problems.

Signal Processors

1. For reverbs, delays, choruses, exciters, equalizers, and so on, try running different types of sounds (steady, percussive, thick, thin) into the inputs at the proper signal levels. Just make sure that the unit is in fact processing, and that level meters and input, output, and mix controls are responding. If there is a MIDI port on the device and you have a sequencer or other MIDI controller handy, try sending MIDI program changes to the unit.

2. For compressors, send a low-level source into the input, and then raise and lower the output level of the compressor to verify that it is affecting the dynamics of the signal. A quick test for a noise gate is to send a steady low-level signal to the input, and then raise the gate threshold until the signal cuts off at the output.

Sound Generators

1. Check the entire keyboard on every synthesizer, controller and workstation for loose or nonfunctional keys.

2. Send the sound generator output to an amplifier and just play, making sure that all sound banks contain the proper presets (especially if you have a demo model). If the original presets have been changed, check the owner's manual—it may be possible to reset the software with a keystroke sequence. If not, the dealer may be able to dump the original SysEx (System-Exclusive) information back into the machine via the MIDI ports.

Power Amplifiers

1. Before testing, be sure to connect the power amp to a proper impedance speaker load.

2. Turn the volume down on all channels before powering up.

3. Feed a steady signal into the inputs and raise volume gradually, just to verify output to all speakers.

Mixing Console

1. Before making any other connections, connect the master send outputs to a monitor source.

2. Using a Line-level input source (or whatever level source the board requires), move from input to input verifying the input signal.

3. Route signals from any given input channel to all the various buses, subgroup outputs, effects sends, and so on. Check that the signal shows up where expected and, just as importantly, that it does not show up anywhere it is not expected. Run through the manual to make sure you cover all the bases here.

4. Repeat this procedure for mike-level inputs, if applicable.

Paperwork

Once you ascertain that a piece is working, fill out the warranty card, stamp it, and get it into the mail. If a device is incomplete in some way, or does not work right out of the box, don't fill out the warranty card. Bring it directly to the dealer's attention. If the dealer tells you to hold onto the unit until a new part comes in, verify that the warranty period will begin at the time the unit is brought into operation, rather than at the time of initial sale, and be sure to secure paperwork from the dealer to that effect.

I had a synchronizer that was useless without a certain connector/cable assembly that had to be ordered from the factory at the time of sale. The synchronizer sat dormant in my studio for six months while I waited for the part. The dealer agreed to write a new receipt when the part came in, so that the warranty period began at that time, and not six months prior.

Next, find a safe place for the instruction manual (preferably a file drawer or box where all manuals will be kept together) and put it there. If you have a copying machine or easy access to one, it is a great idea to make a complete copy of the manual and use that for your day-to-day reference, keeping the original in a secure area. Finally, file your sales receipt, maintenance contracts, and other warranty information for each piece of equipment in an equally secure area.

If you really want to get professional about it, you can set up a maintenance file on each piece of equipment, as many studios do. The file indicates all the cardinal parameters of the machine and describes its anticipated maintenance schedule. The file should contain records of all maintenance, calibration, and repair work performed on the machine, complete with receipts, dealer contracts, warranties, and calibration data sheets. Over the years, it becomes an extremely useful, completely documented history file on the device. For more on this see Chapter 10.

It is good practice to keep a written record of any significant maintenance or repair work that is done on any piece of equipment. Examining these records could point to trends or practices that actually cause equipment to go down. Knowing what was repaired or calibrated when and by whom is good information for tracking down what might have gone wrong with a recording that sounds bad. It is also good for resale purposes to be able to show a record of maintenance on a given machine to a prospective buyer.

Finally, save the box and the packing material if at all possible. I realize that with a studio full of devices, you'll have enough boxes to fill a grain elevator, but for shipping purposes, it's always best to use the box that was intended for the device. Also, when shipping damaged products back to a dealer or manufacturer, you may save yourself the hassle of being blamed for the damage because of your poor packaging.

Installation

All wiring and connectors are labelled and in place. Rack stands have been assembled and spaces are earmarked for each piece of equipment. There is an appropriate number of power outlets available at each rack. You've checked out each device. You have a screwdriver. Begin.

You can install the equipment in any sequence you like; however, it might make some logical sense to hook them up in this sequence:

1. Power amplifiers and monitors.
2. Console.
3. Tape decks.
4. Sound-generating (MIDI) equipment.
5. Outboard processors.

By getting the monitors going and the master sends from the console pumped out to the power amp, you can begin to listen to each connection as it is made. To avoid transient pops or feedback squeals that might tear your speaker cones into confetti, turn down the amplifier volume each time you plug in another device. Turn on the new piece, raise the amplifier levels gradually, and listen.

Sometimes connecting an audio wire to an input or a power cord to a new piece of gear will result in a hum, buzz, or static noise in the audio path. By treating each problem as they come up, you could save hours of detective work that might have to be spent if you first install everything, and then turn it all on at once and listen.

Eliminating Grounding Problems

Here's where things get tricky. If anybody out there installs an entire room full of studio equipment, brings up all the levels and does not hear any unwanted buzzes, hums or hisses, I would appreciate it if you would write to me so that you can become my official hero and mentor. The following is a list of things to check for when you get an audio ground problem:

- Be sure that all grounding-wire terminals in the power wiring of your studio are clean and securely tightened.

- It's usually not too difficult to identify the signal path or paths that are causing ground hum. If you raise and lower the mixer input faders one at a time, you will often notice that certain channels are exhibiting much more noise than others. For example, if all your tape returns are buzzing, it is likely that the tape deck grounding is amiss. If the monitors are buzzing even with all the faders down, you probably have a ground loop at the power amplifier itself.

- Sometimes ground hum is induced rather than conducted (which means your wires pick it up through the air, acting like an antenna). Often, physically relocating or changing the orientation of equipment will reduce or eliminate hum. On equipment with no grounding conductor (2-prong plug), try reversing the plug to determine the best position.

- Once you identify the problem circuits, try to trace the ground path for that equipment. Remember that grounding problems are primarily caused by either a poorly connected main ground or an inadvertent alternate path. Usually the loop is the result of a redundant ground in the power connection or a path through the equipment enclosure into another piece of grounded equipment.

High-Frequency Noise

Sometimes an undesirable high-frequency noise will be present in an audio line, and this is usually the result of electromagnetically induced signals. If you are experiencing this problem, here are some possible remedies:

- Make sure that the ground shield on the audio cable is not connected at both ends. One end should be left open to allow the shield to act as an antenna, with the other end of the shield acting as a "drain" to dump the unwanted signal to ground.

- If the wire run is unbalanced, balance it. See Chapter 5 on wiring procedures.

- If all else fails, try ferrite beads. These are little metal loops that you send your audio wiring through, which seemingly suck the noise right out of the wire. They are available through professional audio supply stores.

System Check

Once everything is screwed in, connected, MIDIed, wiped down and turned on, it's time to start a complete checkout of the studio. It's better to find problems during a maintenance check than during a session.

Also, a rigorous checkout is a good way to get acquainted with the operation of your equipment. This could take several days, so try to be patient and methodical. And by all means, take some time out to record some music if enough equipment is working and the inclination hits you. Along the way you may find some bugs or work out kinks in the system. Just don't forget to continue your formal system check once you get your yah-yahs out.

It helps to create a written checklist, with room for making notes, that you can go through to test every audio path. It doesn't really matter where you begin, as long as you cover everything. Appendix C shows a checklist for Studio B (the order is just one that I thought made sense).

Here are some suggestions for a complete studio checkout:

Console and Multitrack

- Check out all buses and all line inputs.

  Send a steady signal to console line input 1. Determine whether input is present, and then route signal to all sends—stereo bus (try panning left and right), subgroups, auxiliaries, and effect sends—and be sure that the signal appears at each of these. Repeat for all input channels.

- Check out phantom voltage and mike inputs.

  Plug a condenser microphone requiring phantom voltage into each mike input and verify the signal.

- Calibrate Console VUs and check out tape sends.

  Place all channels of multitrack into record mode. Apply a steady signal to all tape sends, and raise subgroup faders (or channel outputs) until the tape deck VU reads 0db at all channels. Adjust each Console subgroup VU until it reads 0db (Check the console manual—analog VU meters usually have a tiny screw hole that will adjust spring tension on the needle; LED VU meters may have a small trimpot that can be adjusted for level).

- Record a steady signal onto all channels of your multitrack, and then play them back to check tape returns and monitor tape inputs.

- Check master functions—talkback, slate, signal generators, and solo bus.

Studio Functions

You'll need a helper for this. Plug a microphone into station 1, pull it up on the console and check for signal. Repeat for all stations. Repeat for line inputs. Send signal from console to all headphone stations and verify.

Patch Bay and Peripheral Equipment

This is simply a matter of trying to route signals to and from every piece of signal processing and sound generating equipment into the console and back. Here are some guidelines:

- If you have a synchronizer, try sending time code to a tape track from the synchronizer, and then reading it back.

- Send MIDI signals to all MIDI devices from the sequencer and make sure that all controllers are sending to the sequencer.

- Check out all special functions on the patch bay, such as mults, half-normals and normals.

- Break into pre-patch and post-patch sends and returns and verify that signals are engaging and normals are disengaging.

Don't panic if a signal doesn't show up where it's supposed to. First, be sure that you are routing correctly in accordance with the proper operating procedures of each device (translated: read the manual again). If everything seems right, check your connectors for cold solder joints or loose connections. In the process of installation, connections often become loose. It's also very easy to inadvertently plug wire number 234 into the jack where wire number 233 belongs. You'll find that you did this when you try to send a signal to the reverb, for example, and it ends up at the compressor.

There is a possibility that signals sent to a given input will appear at numerous other inputs as well. Initially, I found that signals sent to the studio headphone jacks showed up on the studio line inputs and also at the tape sends. This very undesirable situation usually means that there is a common signal ground somewhere where there shouldn't be. It turned out that the signal ground on my power amplifier was conductively connected through the rack rails to various signal inputs at the patch bay. It was pretty embarrassing when the guitar track that was originally recorded to track 4 also showed up later on tracks 7 through 12.

The toughest problems to solve are the ones that don't show up all the time—the transients. This is the sinister high-frequency noise that materializes in the monitors for ten seconds, and then goes away as mysteriously as it appeared. Or the ground buzz that you swear was there yesterday and now that your partner is around to listen to it, it's gone.

Often, these are caused by an appliance or some other type of equipment turning on, dumping electromagnetic noise onto your line and turning off again. Also, ground potential in a large building may change at different times of the day depending on the amount of electricity being used at any given time. Both of these problems are difficult to remedy if the machines causing the trouble are not part of your household or otherwise under your control.

If you can trace the circuit being affected by the electromagnetic noise, you could try installing an EMI filter in the line. This is a special electronic network that filters out electromagnetic interference at a specified design frequency. Check with your local professional audio or electronics dealer for guidance. The grounding problem can be eliminated by using a separate dedicated ground bus for the studio wiring if possible.

Since not everything can be fixed immediately, you'll be generating a list of things that need to be done over time to get the studio into perfect operating condition. The bad news is that the list never seems to go away. There's always a little buzz here or a little glitch there that needs to be dealt with. A door that sticks. A cable that needs replacement. A device that needs repair. Congratulations, you're a studio owner, and this is part of the territory. Try to keep up with this stuff as best you can, otherwise you may find yourself swamped.

Maintenance and Repair

The next logical step is to discuss maintenance and repair. The object here is the preservation of your equipment and the elimination of studio downtime; downtime results in loss of creative possibilities (in a private studio) and loss of money (in a business).

Cleaning the Tape Path

The bulk of the routine maintenance will take place on your tape machines. Remember, these machines have the most moving parts and are most subject to wear and tear of all studio equipment. Become a "clean the tape heads" fanatic. You can't clean the tape heads too often (as long as you're doing it right).

As tape travels past the heads, it deposits little particles of metal oxide (that you can't even see) on the tape heads. These act like mountains and boulders relative to the recording path. The more you let this build up, the worse your recordings will sound, and the more difficult this crud will be to remove.

Heads should be cleaned on all tape decks before each and every session, and after three or four hours of use at a minimum. If you're not sure whether or not to clean the heads, clean the heads. If someone asks, "Should we clean the heads?", clean the heads.

To do this, use a high-quality tape-cleaning fluid (or denatured alcohol) and a tightly wrapped cotton swab available from professional audio shops. Do not use regular Q-Tips, as they are loosely wrapped and may end up depositing more debris on your tape heads than they take off. Also, do not use isopropyl or rubbing alcohol; these contain water (which can cause oxidation) or other ingredients (which can leave deposits).

Clean all areas of the machine that come in contact with the tape, including capstans, rollers, pinchers, and so on. Rub gently in a left-to-right motion, parallel to the tape path. Do not use the tape head cleaning fluid on rubber parts, as it will harden and degrade the rubber. There are special rubber cleaners available for cleaning these parts, or you can simply use warm water.

Demagnetizing

Many tape deck manuals and many audio equipment books will advise you to demagnetize your tape heads on a regular basis. They claim that after many passes, tape heads will gradually develop a magnetic field on them that will erase high-frequency signals from the recording (even in playback mode!). To alleviate this problem, you are told to use a demagnetizer, which is a device that generates a strong magnetic field.

Turn off the machine, turn on the demagnetizer holding it a few feet away from the heads, and then slowly bring the demagnetizer very close to the head surface without touching it, and slowly bring it back to a few feet away. This process should randomize any small magnetic charge on the tape head.

The problem is that if you do it wrong, you can permanently magnetize the head to the point where it is unusable. Yipe! Many recording engineers advise that it is not very good practice to demagnetize your heads on a regular basis. This, they say, is because the amount of magnetic charge that actually deposits on tape heads in normal use is highly overestimated, and the possibility of making a mess of your machine in the process is highly underestimated.

They recommend that you purchase a magnetometer (costs about $50 from electrical supply stores) and periodically measure the charge on the heads. If the charge approaches a value between .3 and .5 gauss, or if your golden ears hear a high-frequency roll off on your recorded material, do the demag thing. Otherwise, leave well enough alone.

Tape Deck Calibration and Nonroutine Adjustments

This stuff begins to get a little scary for those not technically inclined, because you do have to open up the machine and deal with words like azimuth and attenuator. But once you roll up your sleeves and get into an electronic frame of mind, you'll find that this work is simply a matter of following a fixed set of rules.

Some studios do head alignments and electronic calibration on their machines every single morning. This type of maintenance schedule is critical if you routinely work on tapes recorded at other studios or if you send your tapes to other studios for further processing or mixdown.

On the other hand, if your tape decks sound fine to you and you're not overly concerned about compatibility with other people's machines, you can just farm this work out to your local audio dealer or repair shop once or twice a year. The work I'm talking about consists of the following maintenance practices:

- Tape speed adjustment.

- Wow and flutter adjustment.

- Head tilt and azimuth adjustment.

- Input level check.

- Reproduce level check.

- Tape tension adjustment.

Most of this work requires special tools and materials. The following is a list of the minimum necessary items:

- Wow and flutter meter.
- Audio oscillator.
- Digital frequency counter.
- Oscilloscope.
- Spring scale (for checking tape tension).
- Calibrated test tapes.

The procedures to follow for head alignment, wow and flutter measurement, and other calibration work are usually described in detail in the maintenance manual for the machine. The manual will also indicate the proper test tape frequencies and standards. If you have a good relationship with your equipment dealer, you may be able to get someone to run through a set of these operations on the machine for you before you set it up in the studio.

Repair Work

Face it—sooner or later (usually sooner), some critical piece of gear is going to go on strike. Be absolutely certain that it is the device that has malfunctioned, and not the circuitry connected to the device. This is most easily done by connecting some similar device to that circuitry, and verifying that the circuitry does indeed work. For example, if one of your reverb units stops sending signal, remove it and connect another reverb or similar effects device (one you know is working) to the same cables. If you still get no output, you can be relatively certain that it is a cabling or connector problem, and not a problem with the reverb unit.

Once you're convinced that there's something wrong with the machine, check your records. If the warranty or service contract has not expired, don't touch it. Just pack it up in its box (which you saved on delivery day because you pay attention to my every word), and return it to the dealer or the manufacturer—whichever is specified in the warranty or service contract.

If there is no warranty or service contract in effect, you'll have to pay for a repair, and this can get expensive on even the simplest of machines. Heed this warning, however, if you're thinking of doing your own repair work. Unless you have a thorough knowledge of electricity and electrical components, you should not be fooling around inside the enclosure of an electrical device. As expensive as repair work might be, it is usually much cheaper than a hospital bill or a funeral service. Make sure that anyone you hire or bribe to do electrical repair work on the premises of your home or studio is a qualified technician, or you could wind up in a heap of legal trouble.

Smoking

If you can help it, don't let people smoke in your studio. This may bother some clients (and that's a trade-off you'll have to consider), but electronic equipment ionizes the air around it—and attracts tar and nicotine particles like a magnet attracts iron. After a few months of running in a smoke-filled room, you can open up a piece of gear and write your name in the muck that's deposited on all the internal components. This is about as good for the health and longevity of your electronics as it is for your lungs, so if you can avoid it . . . .

Summary

This phase of the studio project is the one in which you actually begin to experience the equipment and the design you worked to achieve. It is important, however, to resist the temptation to just "plug and play," wiring up your various devices without the appropriate preparation and precautionary measures.

Maintenance, testing and troubleshooting—although these are not the most glamorous aspects of studio work, they are among the most important tasks that need to be performed. As with any other discipline, a great deal of pride and satisfaction can be derived from operating a well-tuned and functioning studio. Also, by keeping all your records straight and your paperwork in order, you can avoid hassles and save money on repairs.

10

GOING MULTIMEDIA

Until the last decade or so, the film and video industry didn't care too much about sound. TV was broadcast in mono, and recording studios were subcontracted to produce soundtracks that consisted mostly of voice, with some marginal background music.

The sound recording industry, for that matter, didn't care too much about picture. Serious high-fidelity recording was strictly reserved for music in an album format. Recording artists were sometimes featured in movies or on television, but the sound production was usually pretty dismal. The film industry and the sound recording industry were completely separate entities.

Then came movies recorded in Dolby stereo, VCRs, MTV, and stereo broadcast TV. A revolution occurred—high-quality stereo sound and state-of-the-art picture were totally and irreversibly joined together. Film and video production houses began to add recording studio capabilities to their facilities. Recording studios began to install video monitors, videotape recorders, and synchronization equipment. Pretty soon, it became hard for some places to determine whether they were video production companies or recording studios.

Next came computer animation and imaging, and computer control of both video and audio production. Soon the audio/video facilities were adding computer graphics and control capabilities to their growing arsenal of diversified equipment. Enter the new terminology—multimedia production, defined as the integration of computers, graphics, animation, video, music, speech, and live presentation.

Just about everything you see on TV is now a product of sophisticated multimedia production—from the swirling 3-D graphics and funky theme music of the network ID spots to the wild images and music of MTV to the incredible audio and video special effects in today's blockbuster movies. The good news is that, like recording equipment, the equipment necessary to do some of the most intense multimedia work is becoming economically accessible to the project studio owner.

Multimedia may not be for everyone. Just because you are a musician with a recording studio does not mean that you have to get involved with video or computer graphics. Most of the multimedia work that is done today involves a team of specialists—the computer animation people, the video production people, and the sound and music people.

If you're only interested in audio, many of these teams could use the help of a specialist like yourself. However, if you're interested in multimedia in order to expand your creative endeavors or to make more money by expanding your business, take a ride through this chapter. I'll give a general explanation of the various aspects of multimedia production and the equipment and expertise you need to implement it.

Audio for Video

Many of today's successful studios have been kept alive by the audio for video market, which can be broken down into three categories:

Professional Film and Video Pre- and postproduction for TV commercials, high-end music video postproduction, movie soundtracks, and so on.

Private Sector Industrials Soundtracks and sweetening for corporate training videos, slide shows and computer presentations, and so on. (*Sweetening* refers to the enhancement of the audio portion of a video by adding music or sound effects to the basic recorded dialog.)

Lower Budget Projects Soundtracks for private film or video artists, wedding videos, and so on.

All of the above would require at least minimal video sync capabilities in the studio. At a minimum, the low-end stuff could be done by simply adding a video monitor, VCR, and synchronizer to a basic MIDI setup. The most critical decision, in that case, is the type of video machine you use. Here are your choices, in the order of least to most expensive:

- *Any consumer-grade stereo VHS or Beta VCR*—Since the video is only for reference purposes, and the quality of the picture is not important while doing audio work, you can get away with a consumer deck in many cases. After the audio tracks are completed, they can be dubbed onto the professional video master at another facility.

- *Super VHS or "High-8" format VCR*—These machines, though not quite "broadcast quality," have superior picture characteristics and transport functions when compared to consumer VCRs. For lower-budget video productions, this format can sometimes be used as the final product. (High-8 is a very new format that is becoming popular in professional circles for its extremely good picture quality.)

- *3/4-inch VTR*—If you intend to deal with commercial video production houses, it may be necessary to use a commercial-grade videotape recorder running 3/4-inch tape. These are very sophisticated machines; many have time-code-controllable transports and other professional features. They are much more expensive than the other formats mentioned in this list. It may be possible, however, to obtain a used 3/4-inch machine for roughly the cost of a new Super VHS deck.

At the other end of the spectrum is *postproduction*. This is the process by which the many different camera angles and visual cuts are edited together to form a (sometimes) coherent end product. In modern "post" work, nearly all the sounds associated with the picture are added at this time, also.

Successful postproduction requires very sophisticated synchronization systems, hard-disk-based recording, automated mixer functions, extensive sound effects libraries, and more. Complex postproduction often involves setting up hundreds of *sound cues* on multitrack tape machines (and/or hard disk recording systems) and syncing them to picture.

Consider an action-packed movie scene in which there are street sounds, guns, cars, sirens, voices, footsteps (left and right), helicopters, screams, and music all being placed in the film after the fact from sound effects libraries. A fifteen-second sequence might include hundreds of sounds which must be synced, EQed, dynamically panned in the stereo field, and mixed. It's a big job.

Synchronization

Synchronization is by far the most critical aspect of audio for video. In a minimal setup such as the one shown in Figure 10.1, the consumer-grade VCR would have to be used as the master time code device, since its transport functions are not sophisticated enough to be driven by time code fed from the synchronizer. The synchronizer reads time code from the videotape, and controls various sound-generating devices such as the multitrack tape deck and the MIDI sequencer.

This basic system could be used to generate audio tracks that would sync to a previously edited videotape. To control the other equipment, the videotape would also have to be provided with time code—which brings us to a very brief discussion on SMPTE time code.

SMPTE Time Code

There are different types of codes used for synchronization, such as MIDI time code, SMPTE time code, and a host of others. For video production (even if you are using MIDI), SMPTE is the one you are most concerned with.

There are two different ways of stripping and reading SMPTE time code—Longitudinal Time Code (LTC) and Vertical Interval Time Code (VITC). LTC goes down on an audio track of the VCR, just like it does on a multitrack tape recorder. VITC is superimposed onto the video frame of the videotape in an area that cannot be seen by the viewer, and is independent of the audio track.

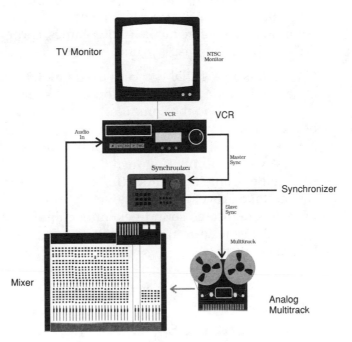

Figure 10.1 A minimal setup for audio-video synchronization.

If you're going to do video sync, it's best to get a synchronizer that can read both LTC and VITC. By reading VITC off the master, you can leave the audio tracks free to dub the soundtrack onto them. Otherwise, you have to use one track of audio for the LTC. Unless you have a VCR with center-track time code (essentially a 3 track audio circuit), you won't be able to lay down stereo.

The other alternative is to get all your audio tracks recorded and synced to the video using your basic VCR and LTC time-code reader. Then, as mentioned above, bring the completed master (with time code) over to a video facility for "layback" onto the 1-inch video master.

Other Audio

Audio for video is just one subset of the possibilities for audio in multimedia. There is also a lot of work going on in audio production for computer-interactive media (video games, corporate presentations, interactive advertising displays, and so on).

In this area, MIDI is a very useful tool. If the music for a computer-controlled multimedia production were recorded digitally (the way CDs are) and placed on the computer's hard disk, it would take up 10 megabytes of memory per minute of music. To process this information would also eat up a great deal of the computer's processor time. To save memory space—while still offering incredible audio quality and sound effects—some video game companies (for example) are putting MIDI sound files (which take up very small amounts of memory) into the software—and including dedicated sound-generator chips in the hardware. (These chips are similar to those used in studio synthesizers—and are, in effect, "played" by the software.)

Video Standards

In North America, there is a video standard called NTSC. This ensures that VCRs, cameras, broadcasts, and so on are 100% compatible. NTSC dictates a 30-frame-per-second frame rate—actually 29.97 frames per second—each frame consisting of 525 lines of 910 pixels (dots of color). Some of the lines are used for synchronization, so the image resolution is actually about 484 by 746. If you've heard all the talk about High Definition Television (HDTV), it represents a proposed higher image-resolution standard. Europe and South America use a completely different system (called PAL) which is not compatible with NTSC.

For those of you who might be interested in video editing using multiple picture sources, be aware that video signals cannot be mixed as easily as audio. They must first be synchronized to a common sync source. This is known as *gen-locking*. Video decks also exhibit erratic signal timing due to their mechanical transports; this means that when you try to control one video machine with another, the picture may become distorted. For mixing, switching, or editing, the output of each video deck must be stabilized using a *Time Base Corrector* (TBC). (TBCs cost between $800 and $1600 each.)

Because nothing is ever simple, the signals of computer displays are quite different from that of standard video. Specialized hardware is needed to display computer graphics and animation on an NTSC monitor. Computers typically use a pixel display system known as RGB, which stands for Red Green Blue. By properly combining these three colors, any one of 16.7 million colors can be generated. (Note, however, that the actual ability to generate and display these colors is dependent upon the system.) Typical resolution is approximately 640 by 480 pixels.

Video from an external source can be converted to RGB format and displayed on a computer monitor using a video capture board. However, this is a simple system that does not allow the computer to manipulate or store the image. To do that, the image must be *digitized* (converted to digital information that can be read by the computer)—a much more complicated task.

It is possible to do rather intricate video graphics and animation on a desktop computer. Ideally, however, the computer would have to be a high-end system with lots of hard disk space (100+ megabytes), lots of RAM (at least 5 megabytes), and fast clock speed. This is because video is memory-intensive, and the software required to perform 3-D graphics and animation is extremely complex.

Also, to do sophisticated graphics, you would need a reasonably good-sized RGB monitor—19 inches or larger is preferred. As you may have guessed, the 19-inch monitor you purchased for your NTSC video setup won't work with the computer—it's not compatible. There are monitors designed to work with both NTSC and RGB inputs, but I have found that these actually cost more than two separate monitors—one RGB and one NTSC. Perhaps as the call for dual-purpose monitors increases, the price of these units will come down.

Recently, some breakthroughs have been made in the field of computer and video processing hardware and software. A device called the

Video Toaster by Newtek can perform animation, video editing, titling, graphics and video special effects rivalling those of the best TV production houses—at a cost of roughly $5000. Other similar devices are in development at this time that will probably bring the world of video production out of the multimillion-dollar production suite and onto the desktop computer.

This is pretty exciting stuff—especially if you happen to own an audio project studio. For a small investment, you can turn your recording operation into a multimedia service capable of generating super-high-quality audio/video presentations, commercials, displays, or just plain art.

What's Next?

Given the speed at which technology is progressing, it's hard to predict what the future will bring. In the case of multimedia, it appears that the term *interactive* is the buzzword for the future. Audio/Video programs that respond to input from the listener/viewer are under development and promise to become an exciting new part of our lives. Video games, interactive television, sophisticated educational tools, interactive art— these represent the cutting edge in the industry. My guess is that the private artists—the project studio users—will be the primary suppliers of innovation in this area.

This chapter is just an overview of what it takes to get into this kind of work. For more detailed information on audio and video techniques, I have listed some books in Appendix A.

THE STUDIO BUSINESS

There are entire books devoted to this subject, so this chapter is only intended to give an overview of the considerations necessary to initiate a recording business and hopefully get you off to a smooth start. Before making the decision to go into business, be sure to clarify your responsibilities under the local zoning laws, as described later in this chapter.

Remember, the benefits of owning a private studio are obvious to a practicing musician or songwriter, but not everyone is cut out for the recording studio business. In some areas (New York, Los Angeles, and Nashville, to name a few), it is highly competitive—the number of studios can almost be measured in terms of studios per square mile. Naturally, price wars are common, and profit margins at the small-studio level are not what they used to be 10 or 20 years ago.

On the positive side, there are new niches in the recording industry that did not exist 20 years ago. These have been created by the insurgence of video, coupled with technical breakthroughs in MIDI sequencing and digital sampling. Add to this the fact that for young people, learning to play an instrument and putting a band together seems to be about as common today as being on a little league baseball team. This means there's a lot more pie to be divided up as well.

Zoning Laws

Many residential zoning laws prohibit the use of homes for commercial business. The primary reason for zoning laws is that people do not want their quiet neighborhoods turned into commercial areas with clients coming and going at all hours, cars parked up and down the street, people milling about outside, and so on. Zoning laws also require that commercial businesses offering public access meet strict building codes dealing with parking, access for the handicapped, fire prevention, safety features, and other considerations that the average home studio owner might not be in a position to provide.

There is a great deal of controversy surrounding the issue of using home studios for commercial purposes. The owners of professional recording studios argue that home studios are competing unfairly because they do not incur the same expenses associated with building codes in commercial areas. This may be a legitimate gripe. Beware: If you are operating a home studio in an area that is not zoned for it, and you are advertising studio time to the general public, you may find a local building inspector at your door acting on a complaint from a commercial studio in town. If the inspector finds that you are indeed operating in violation of the law, you will be ordered to cease operation.

You may apply for a *zoning variance* (an exception to the zoning rule based on special circumstances). This involves a local hearing of the zoning board, of which all of your neighbors living within a certain radius of your home will be notified and given the opportunity to support or reject your request for variance. It is recommended that you hire a lawyer if you decide to apply for a zoning variance.

Home studio owners argue that the line between commercial use and private use of a studio is not clearly defined. If you use your home studio only to write and produce your own music, you are operating legally. However, if that music ends up being sold commercially (for example, if it becomes a hit record), you are technically in violation of most residential zoning laws. Home studio proponents also point out that federal tax laws have been set up to promote the use of the home for business purposes through tax breaks, but many zoning laws conflict with this.

Whichever side of this issue you sympathize with, be sure to clarify your particular situation before going ahead with a commercial business venture.

The Business Plan

I realize it sounds bureaucratic, but as a business owner, you should develop a written business plan. Doing without it is sort of like walking up to the line of scrimmage in a football game without knowing what play was called. Chances are you'll be in for some unpleasant surprises.

The main advantage of preparing a business plan is to focus your own thoughts on how the business will be run. It forces you to think about the many variables associated with the business, especially the ones you don't want to think about—like risks and competition. The plan will prompt you to reflect on how you will market your business, who you are going to consider your customers and how you intend to service them. It requires you to come up with a pricing scheme and generate projected income figures.

If you take the time to work out the plan seriously, you will find it can be used as an effective way to gauge your progress as you go along. Also, if you apply for a business loan, either now or sometime in the future, the plan can be submitted to the financial institution for evaluation.

Appendix B contains a sample business plan that you can use as a model for your own plan. It contains examples and advice about how to fill out the plan for your own studio.

The Small Business Development Center

If you have a Small Business Development Center in your area, take advantage of its services. Most SBDC services are free—paid for by the taxes you'll undoubtedly pay if your studio makes a lot of money. They will assist you in developing a business plan, preparing advertising material and promotional campaigns, and perhaps even obtaining financial assistance. The office of the SBDC usually has information available on the legal and practical aspects of running a business, such as organizational structure, price setting, publicity, loan information assistance, accounting, and small business start-ups.

To Incorporate or Not To Incorporate

From a legal and structural standpoint, there are three primary ways to set up a business. Which one you choose will depend upon your personal circumstances.

Sole Proprietorship

This is by far the simplest option. Decide what you are going to do and how you are going to do it (by generating a business plan), and then fill out a state registration form indicating that you are *DBA*, which stands for *Doing Business As* (lawyers are into acronyms, too). The forms will help you decide whether or not you have to charge sales tax. If you have employees, the federal government will send you more forms to fill out on a periodic basis.

You need to set up your own bookkeeping ledger, and open a single bank account under the business name through which all monies will pass. This gives you an additional account of all your business transactions. Taxes are relatively easy to decipher—there is a form called the "Profit (or Loss) from Business or Profession (Sole Proprietorship) Schedule C 1040," that you file along with your personal income tax.

The main disadvantage to a sole proprietorship is that you are personally liable for any claims against the business. There are also certain expenses that you cannot deduct from your business income, such as medical and dental insurance, life insurance, and so on.

Partnerships

This is also relatively simple and inexpensive, if you work everything out in advance with your partners. You may take on partners for financial reasons, for their expertise, or both. You should decide among yourselves what each person's input is worth, and what duties and responsibilities will be incurred by each individual. Translate this to a percentage share of the business (50/50, 20/40/40, whatever). This should all be spelled out in writing in a *partnership agreement* and signed by all. Standard-form partnership agreements are available at legal stationery suppliers, and make very good guides. However, the final document should be reviewed by an attorney prior to signing.

The operating mechanisms of the partnership are similar to those of the sole proprietorship, in that each partner is personally liable for the business as well as the liabilities incurred by the other partners as part of doing business. Each partner will file two tax returns, an individual income tax return (Form 1040) and Form 1065.

Corporations

There are two types of corporations: the Subchapter S corporation and the C corporation.

The *Subchapter S corporation* might be a good idea for a small studio business because it is treated as an individual for tax purposes. This means you can deduct certain expenses and losses from a Subchapter S corporation against your personal earned income (which you can't do in a C corporation). Subchapter S also protects you from certain liabilities and negligence claims, since only the corporation can be named in a suit, not the individual.

The downside? It costs roughly $400 to $500 to incorporate (and that's if you do it without the help of a lawyer). Also, there's more bookkeeping required, which means that your yearly or monthly accounting expenses may go up. Finally, based on the amount of money you make, you may pay more in taxes under a Subchapter S arrangement than you would under a sole proprietorship. Do your homework before you make a decision on this. Consult with a business accountant, using your projections from the business plan to estimate expenses and income.

Finally, there is the *C corporation*. This structure gives you the most advantage in terms of limited liability, ease in doing business from one corporation to another, lower taxes (if your corporate profit is under

$50,000 annually), pension benefits, medical insurance and fringe benefits, and so on. The disadvantages are more paperwork, a higher formation charge ($500 to $1000), and higher accounting costs. There is also a requirement that you "act" like a corporation—hold regular board meetings, appoint officers, and so on. If you don't, creditors could claim that you really are partnership in disguise, and push to hold the owners personally liable for the debts of the corporation.

Taxes

Of course, Uncle Sam will be interested in whatever money changes hands at your new facility. I highly recommend that you hire a professional accountant to handle your taxes once the business has been established. The law places certain responsibilities on business owners that you may not be accustomed to if you have never had a business. Unlike working for someone else's company, nobody is going to automatically withhold tax money from your studio revenue. Businesses are required to prepay taxes (based on yearly projected business income) on a quarterly basis. If you don't, you'll be hit with a nasty fine later.

Another consideration is the collection of sales tax in those states where sales tax is applicable. You may be required to collect sales tax on items such as tape or computer disks that you might sell to your customers. This requires you to obtain a *tax number*, which allows you to purchase those items for your inventory without paying sales tax; however, you'll have to keep accurate records of the sales of those items and forward all collected monies to the government.

Advertising

I once saw a write-up on the benefits of advertising that went something like this:

"A man wakes up in the morning and brushes his teeth with an *advertised* toothpaste, washes himself with *advertised* soap, drinks a cup of *advertised* coffee and watches a TV program laced with *advertisements*. He jumps into his *advertised* car, drives past roadside *advertisements* on his way to his business, which he says will do fine without having to *advertise*. Some time later the business fails, and he promptly *advertises* it for sale."

You get the picture.

There are many ways to advertise, and nearly all of them cost money. The trick is to determine which ways will bring in the most return on your investment in terms of business revenue. For a project studio, it will depend on your target audience. Will you be dealing with businesses, other corporations, or advertising agencies? Or are you interested in recording local bands, songwriters, or independent artists? It's too expensive (and perhaps too demanding) to target all possible audiences at the outset, so the best strategy is to decide on a direction and aim your advertising accordingly.

Take a look at where your competitors are advertising. Are they all in the same magazine? Chances are that's a good magazine to advertise in. Look at the Yellow Pages to see where the studios that do your type of work are listed, and what types of ads they take out.

Press Releases

Once you've decided on your target market, create a press release and send it to any and every publication, radio station, or other media entity that might be interested in the opening of a studio or production company. Use your company letterhead if you have one; put the words "Press Release" at the top center of the page, and the words "For Immediate Release" at the top right.

Keep the length down to one page of copy, with most of the pertinent who, what, where, when, and why information in the first one or two paragraphs. Stick to the facts; do not editorialize and do not include opinions. This is a news story. Tell the world about your new business; give good, clear information on the capabilities of both the equipment and the staff. If your project studio looks impressive, including a photograph of the facility might help.

Magazines and Publications

It may be difficult to determine the right publication to advertise in. Unfortunately, placing a single ad in one issue of a periodical does not give you an indication of the effectiveness of the ad. It will take several issues before you can gauge whether or not the ad is effective. Many publications will offer a much lower price on advertising space if you sign a contract to advertise for a minimum number of issues. If, after a considerable amount of time, response to the ad is poor, you have to try to determine whether the fault lies in the publication or the advertising copy itself.

Advertising Agencies

Consider contacting an advertising agency. It may be possible to exchange services here. Find an agency that regularly books studio time for radio spots or whatever, and then offer them free time in return for their services marketing your business. You'll have to pay for material costs, advertising space in publications, air time, and so on, but you'd have to pay for that anyway, and with the expertise of an ad agency on your side, you may come up with a much better campaign.

Direct-Mail Marketing

Direct-mail marketing is not a substitute for other advertising and promotions; it should be used concurrently. One supports the other. The tough part is getting a mailing list that concentrates on your particular target audience. One of the local music papers in our area puts out a yearly list of all the bands in this area, complete with address and contact information. This was an excellent source for a direct mail campaign. If you're after corporate business, it may be more difficult to put together a list. If you know which companies you want to mail to, but don't have a specific name of a person, call the company and ask for the name of their advertising director or corporate communications person. After mailing to a select group, follow up with a phone call: "Did you get my letter? Are you interested?" You never know.

Public Relations

Unless you're a criminal, it pays to keep a high profile. Recording studios are fascinating places, and to the general populace, they conjure up images of Michael Jackson or Frank Sinatra dropping by to create a song or two on a Friday afternoon. Although audio types may know better, there is no need to dispel this image. You might take advantage of the interesting work you do by giving classes on recording at a nearby college or university, or adult education program. There are personal rewards associated with teaching your craft, and you might be able to cultivate clients for your business. Volunteer to give presentations to special interest groups such as library club gatherings, children's centers, lodges, and so on. This is all publicity, and it serves a community purpose as well.

Pricing

To me, this is the most difficult aspect of the business—determining what your services are worth. You can underprice yourself just as easily as you can overprice yourself. I read about a wine distributor who imported a dry, red Spanish wine at a retail cost of about $3.50 per bottle. Its quality rivalled that of French wines priced over $15 per bottle. The problem was nobody was buying it. After raising the price of the Spanish wine to about $8.00 per bottle, the stuff sold like wildfire. The moral is, if you charge too little, you will be sending a message to people—either that you don't consider yourself worth more, or that others won't pay more for your services. Also, your objective here is to make money, not just to attract clients. You could be booked solid, but barely covering your expenses.

On the other hand, it will be difficult to attract clients while charging the same hourly rate for your project studio as that of the multimillion-dollar facility down the block. Difficult at first, anyway, because it is quite possible that both your service and your end product are comparable in quality to that of the multimillion-dollar facility, and the charges are justifiable.

A good way to start is to call all the studios in your area, make like a prospective client, and find out what they are offering in terms of services and fees. Most studios charge an hourly rate and a lockout fee, which is a reduced rate for clients interested in booking the studio for a significant amount of time (for example, all day, one week, and so on.) It is also a good incentive to offer block rates for multiple-hour bookings that could be spread out over time. For example, the client might pay in advance for 30 hours of time at a reduced rate, and then book the time as his or her schedule allows.

Terms and Conditions

This brings me to the very important topic of dealing with clients. Given the chance, many clients will take you for a long bumpy ride at your expense. It is important to set up ground rules from the outset and make sure the people you are working with understand them.

Booking Policy

Set a *minimum advance notice* for cancellation of bookings to discourage clients from cancelling sessions at the last minute. You should require a deposit up front to reserve time, otherwise you really have no recourse against the client that cancels on short notice. At the same time, it might not pay to be too inflexible. You may decide to waive the deposit for steady clients, or not to charge a good client for an emergency cancellation. Gestures such as these make for return business.

Studio Time

You must decide how to handle back-to-back bookings. Do you leave a half hour between sessions for the inevitable run over time, cleanup and/or setup for the next session, a short rest for the recording staff (which is probably you)? It is annoying to most clients to have the next band or producer milling about in the studio during the last half hour of their session, and it is also annoying for the next band to arrive a few minutes early and have to wait outside. Clients should also be notified that regardless of what time they arrive, the studio clock begins at the time of booking; in other words, they cannot book for eight o'clock, then show up at 9:00 and expect to pay from nine o'clock.

You may notice that certain clients invariably need more time than they book to finish sessions. Eventually you might automatically skip a few hours between sessions to accommodate this situation. Of course, the client cannot be held liable for that time if he or she does not use it. A better approach might be to suggest reserving more hours when the session is booked.

There is another side to this time coin. The studio usually starts charging money as soon as the client walks in the door. It is considered fair and appropriate to charge clients for the time that is spent setting up the band's equipment, getting the proper drum sounds, and otherwise adjusting the studio for the type of recording that the particular client requires.

However, some studios will take that a step further and perform routine (or major) maintenance and repair work on studio equipment while the client is on the clock. I'm not talking about head cleaning—I'm talking about resoldering patchbay connections, tracking down ground loops, reconfiguring machine outputs, and so on. Most clients will not appreciate being charged for this kind of thing, and I don't blame them. It may be necessary to perform the repair work before the session can begin, but I don't think the client should be paying for downtime.

Another ploy on the part of some studios is to take an inordinately long time to achieve a desired sound or effect. In another studio, I watched one day as a singer asked for a different sounding reverb on her voice, and the engineer sat for one-and-a-half hours tweaking the reverb unit until he thought it was right. The client was exasperated, and should have said something, but the end result was that she never set foot in that studio again.

Payment

Most studios work on a pay as you go basis. Some will require half of the total in advance to reserve the time, and then collect the balance at the end of the session. Others establish a billing rapport with clients and simply send the bill in the mail after a session. The latter approach is OK for dealing with advertising agents and industry people; however, private artists and bands are a little less likely to pay promptly by mail, and a lot harder to track down when they don't. My suggestion when dealing with local bands and songwriters is, "Pay as you leave or you don't get a tape."

Bids

Some companies seeking audio production services for radio or television will send out requests for bids. The request will indicate the scope of the project and the type of work involved. The first (and most difficult) task in this situation is to become one of the facilities that receives such a request. I'm not sure how much guidance I can give you in this matter, except that—as mentioned earlier—you should keep a high profile and keep your ears open.

If you eventually do receive a request for bid, you will have to prepare a cost estimate based on the information in the bid request, indicate the time frame in which you will complete the work, enclose a resume or demo tape highlighting your incredible talents, and pray that you get the job. Whether or not you get the job will depend on how well you market yourself in the demo, and how low your price was compared to the other bidders, usually not in that order.

Again, don't sell yourself short just to get the job. If you underbid, thinking that it will get your foot in the door, and then you can raise the price on the next project, you're headed for a bad situation. Aside from the fact that you will work and not make any money from it, contractors can sniff that sort of thing out pretty easily, and will usually gravitate in another direction.

The bid that you generate is binding. You must perform the work at that price (as long as the actual amount of work remains as stated in the request), and you must deliver on time, or at best you will never see that client again, and at worst there may be legal action taken against you.

Determining Your Limitations

In the fortunate event that your studio begins to see a lot of business, you've got to be careful not to spread yourself too thin. Recording requires a lot of concentration and effort on the part of the recording engineer, and some producers will push you to the limit of your patience and ability. After a gruelling eight-hour session with a finicky client, you are not likely to be able to perform well for the fresh band of maniacs that is booked for the next eight hours. Book sessions further apart or hire an assistant. If you don't, you'll find yourself inadvertently erasing tracks (something every engineer does at one time or another), taking shortcuts around quality (Producer: "Should we take that track over again?" Exhausted Engineer: "Nahhhhh. Sounds great."), and eventually losing business.

This brings me to quality. Quality in a recording studio is not simply defined as a good tape. It is a mixture of the performance of the equipment, the expertise of the staff, and the atmosphere in the studio itself. Not everyone wants to record in a studio that runs its sessions like a military operation, regardless of how sophisticated or state of the art the facility is. If the studio environment is relaxed and friendly, the artists will play better, the recordings will sound better, and the clients will return.

Nearly every new client who comes into my studio has been in a recording studio before. There is usually only one reason why they did not go back to their original studio: some aspect of quality was lacking there. Very rarely is it because the other studio was too expensive. Either the tape didn't sound good, the atmosphere was disturbing or not conducive to a good performance, or the studio simply did not appear to care about its clients.

Don't forget who's paying the bills here. Many artists will come into the studio and lounge around, warming up, tuning up, drinking, cavorting, and seemingly doing anything but recording. This is their prerogative. It is a mistake to think that you can do the same.

I learned this when a client who often used the studio stopped booking time. Every time this client came in, he would spend about 40 minutes tuning his instrument or warming up his voice. After a while, I found this rather boring and would sometimes pop up a tic-tac-toe game on the computer screen while he was doing his thing. I found out later that this bothered the client immensely; it gave him the impression that I was not interested in his work. Regardless of how disorganized your clients seem to be, they are paying for your time, and you should remain on your toes throughout the session.

Epilogue

After reading this book, it may seem to you that putting a project studio together is quite a task, and you are correct. It is best reserved for those who find the rigors of quality recording to be a labor of love. There were times when my family and friends threatened to set fire to the whole thing, and other times when I was ready to set fire to it myself.

You will be successful if you realize that the studio is not an end in itself, but a means to an end. It is a tool for the creative artist, and completion of your studio construction is merely the beginning of the adventure. If you're like most of the people involved in recording, your payoff will be measured not in terms of how much money you make, but in terms of the finished material that your studio generates over the years. I take great pleasure in listening to many (if not all) of the projects that have been done in my studio, and reflecting on the nearly unimaginable cross section of talented people that I have been privileged to work with.

Not to downplay the money thing, however. Making money by taking part in the creation of music is a great experience—it sort of validates you as an artist (and no matter how much of a techno-head you are, if you take an active part in any audio production, you are an artist.) Shortly after the completion of my project studio, I engineered a radio jingle session for an advertising company. The producer came in with a product to sell, and the rudiments of an idea for the music in his head. During the course of the day, we—the producer, myself, and the various musicians—added our collective ingredients to the production, and the song began to grow and take shape. The finished product was excellent, and it was exhilarating to listen to the final mix. At the end of all this fun, the producer handed me a check in payment for the day's work, and I immediately felt that the studio and all my efforts, lessons learned, hard knocks, anxiety and sweat were being acknowledged. The studio was not some whimsical flight of fancy; it was a real service, to be utilized by people with talent and vision.

To anyone who follows through, I salute you, and I hope that my experience has made for a smoother journey.

RESOURCES

The following magazines and publications are excellent resources for product information and articles on studio design and construction:

db Magazine
Sagamore Publishing Co., Inc.
203 Commack Rd.
Suite 1010
Commack, N.Y. 11725

Electronic Musician
Act III Publishing
6400 Hollis St. #12
Emeryville, CA 94608

EQ
P.S.N. Publications
2 Park Avenue
Suite 1820
New York, N.Y. 10016

Home and Studio Recording
Music Maker Publications, Inc.
21601 Devonshire St.
Suite 212
Chatsworth, CA 91311

Journal of the Audio Engineering Society
Audio Engineering Society
60 East 42nd Street
New York, New York 10075

Mix Magazine
Act III Publishing
6400 Hollis St., #12
Emeryville, CA 94608
Overland Park, KS 66282

R*E*P: Recording Engineering Production
Intertec Publishing Corporation
9221 Quivira
Overland Park, KS 66782

Bibliography

Anderson, Craig. *Home Recording For Musicians*, GPI Publications, 1978.

"The ART Diffusor," (Brochure), Systems Development Group.

Bartlett, Bruce. *Introduction to Professional Recording Techniques*, Howard W. Sams and Co., 1987.

Burger, Jeff. "Making Multimedia," *Electronic Musician*, November 1991.

Cooper, Michael. "The Ins and Outs of Patchbays," *Home and Studio Recording*, November 1991.

Everest, F. Alton. *Handbook of Multichannel Recording*, Tab Books, 1975.

Everest, F. Alton. *The Master Handbook of Acoustics*, Second Edition, Tab Books, Inc., 1989.

Everest, F. Alton and Mike Shea. *How to Build a Small Budget Recording Studio*, Second Edition, Tab Books, Inc., 1988.

Giddings, Phillip. *Audio System Design and Installation*, Howard W. Sams and Co., 1990.

Gorder, Cheryl. *Home Business Resource Guide*, Blue Bird Publishing, 1989.

Huber, David Miles. *Audio Production Techniques For Video*, Howard W. Sams and Co., 1989.

Mead, Judson. *Walls, Floors and Ceilings*, Creative Homeowner Press, 1984.

Morrison, Bill. "Staggered Geometry Designs," *Mix Magazine*, August 1991.

Parson, Mary Jane. *Managing the One Person Business*, Dodd, Mead and Co., 1987.

Peavey A.M.R. Productions Series Console Manual, Peavey Corporation.

Petraglia, David. *The Compleat Watchdog's Guide to Installing Your Own Home Burglar Alarm*, Prentice Hall, Inc., 1984.

Rona, Jeffrey. *Synchronization From Reel to Reel*, Hal Leonard Publishing Corp., 1990.

"RPG Diffusers," (Brochure), RPG Diffusor Systems.

St. Croix, Stephen. "Purple Reign," *Mix Magazine*, August 1991.

Tascam MSR 16 Service Manual, Tascam Corporation.

Way, J. T. "DAWs of Perception," *EQ Magazine*, October 1991.

SAMPLE BUSINESS PLAN

On the next few pages, I'll walk you through a hypothetical business plan for a small project studio (I'll call it Hypothetical Productions). Some of the ideas and technical terms mentioned in the plan are discussed in Chapter 11—so read this chapter before actually completing the plan.

Example entries for Hypothetical Productions' Business Plan will be in italics, and I have included advice for each section where necessary.

The title page and summary information can be used as a quick overview for anyone looking over the plan for the first time. Much of the information presented is repeated in more detail in the body of the plan.

The Three-Year Business Plan

Business plan for: *Hypothetical Productions*

Prepared by:

Date:

Summary

1. Give the name of the business, its location, and description of its physical facilities.

Hypothetical Productions

15 Tumbleweed Way

Dry Gulch, Wyoming

HP is an audio production company specializing in writing and producing soundtracks for movies and television, radio commercials, industrial soundtracks, jingles, and voice overs. Facilities include a 16-track analog multitrack recorder, 32-input console, full MIDI suite with various sound generating equipment, synchronization to video, mixdown to digital audio tape and 1/4-inch 2 track open-reel tape.

2. Briefly describe the product or service.

Hypothetical Productions uses the talents of various musicians, producers, and recording engineers to compose, arrange, and record high-quality audio tracks.

3. What market (for example, consumer, industrial, or government) are you serving? What is unique about this business?

HP is geared toward commercial production for the advertising industry, and for private industry communications. HP also does production work for individual recording artists and songwriters, using a full complement of musical instruments and equipment to create CD-quality recordings at limited cost. The facilities utilize current technology to keep overhead costs low while delivering a high-quality product.

4. What are the overall goals of the business? Who are the people connected with the business?

The goal of Hypothetical Productions is to provide the advertisers and independent artists of the community with previously-unaffordable quality in audio production. The goal is also to use company profits to expand into multimedia operations, offering video, audio, and computer graphics capabilities under one roof.

HP uses a network of musicians, voice-over talent, producers, and other skilled personnel to create any style of production required by the client.

Purpose

The purpose of this prospectus is . . .

Whatever your purpose happens to be—for example, to define the goals and capabilities of your business, to apply for a small business loan, or to propose the business plan to prospective investors.

Table of Contents

Fill in the table of contents after the business plan is completed. Be certain to show page numbers. Make the table of contents a separate page in the plan.

I. The Business

A. Business Description

1. Name:

2. Location:

3. Physical Facilities:

Briefly describe your facility, including the number of rooms, the size of each (in square feet), other amenities (lounge, private jet service, whatever). Then give some information on equipment but be brief—a complete equipment list will be generated later on in the plan.

B. *Products or Services*

1. Description of Product Line

Indicate exactly what your business does and the services you offer.

2. Proprietary Considerations

Describe how your business is set up. Is it a sole proprietorship, a partnership, or a corporation? How many owners or partners are there? Indicate how shares are split or percentage of ownership if applicable. If there are private investors or financial institutions with claim to the facility, indicate those parties.

C. *Management Plan*

1. Organizational Form and Structure

Describe the organization of the company. Are there officers or people designated with certain responsibilities? Define the roles of each.

2. Résumés of Key People

Give full résumés of all business partners and associates. Include education, background, and relevant experience of each person. (This may be a good way to find out a few things you never knew about the people you're working with—"Gee, you have a Ph.D. in Nuclear Waste Disposal?" You never know when stuff like that may come in handy.)

3. Staffing Plan

Do you intend to hire employees? If so, how many and what will their responsibilities be? If you do not intend to hire immediately, but foresee staffing within the first three years of operation, indicate this.

4. Support Services

You may not have all of these people supporting you, but for those you do use, give their names and addresses.

Attorney:
Accountant:
Consultant:
Insurance Agent:
Advertising Agency:
Graphic Designer:
Equipment Suppliers:
Rental Agencies:

D. Operations Plan

1. Facilities and Equipment:

List physical facilities, number of rooms, square footage, acoustic treatments, special wiring, and so on. Provide a complete equipment list including all company assets over $100 in value. This list may become considerable; however, it will be a good reference for you in the event of termination or sale of the business, insurance claims, expansion plans, and so on.

2. Plans for Growth and Expansion

Will you reinvest revenue to expand the business? If so, what percentage of net earnings will be invested? What types of expansion are anticipated? For example, will your facilities be upgraded to include multimedia production work? Will more sophisticated equipment be purchased in an effort to draw higher paying clients?

3. Overall Schedule

When was your business started, or when will it be started? When will construction be completed? Indicate the exact time frame for all work to date and future work anticipated.

4. Process Description

Give a clear rundown on how the product or service is provided. Who initiates contact? Is there preproduction or planning involved in each project? Describe a typical production schedule. How many people are involved? What materials are necessary? What outside services are necessary?

E. Risks

Be realistic here. This is for your own benefit. List each risk with an item number next to it. Include things like the effects of competition, breakthroughs in technology, economic recession, home recording replacing commercial recording businesses, high capital outlays, conflicts of interest or anything else you can think of.

II. Marketing Plan

A. Marketing Research

1. Description of the Market

Are you intending to cater to local thrash metal bands or corporate communications executives? What is the size of your market at this time? Do you have clients waiting or have certain parties expressed interest in your business? Is there a particular group that requires this type of service in your area?

2. Industry Trends

What's going on in this industry now? Is there some new angle that makes you think this is a good time to start this type of business? Usually, with recording studios, the newest trends are based on technology updates. Try to describe those trends and look at how you fit into the picture.

3. Target Market

What type of individuals are you targeting? What captures their attention? Are they industry "suits," are they funky creative "artsy" types, are they technical buffs? What age groups will you deal with?

4. Competition

List each competitor, their name and address, and any other information you can find out about them. Who uses them, what they charge, what equipment they have, the areas they concentrate on, where they advertise. There may be many studios in your area, but not all of them will be your competition. The kind of studio that charges $350 per hour, uses a multimillion-dollar facility, and operates on a yearly capital budget approaching that of Bolivia is not likely to be in competition with a small project studio. A couple of guys in a corrugated tin shack outfitted with a dictaphone and a car stereo system for monitoring might not be stepping into your market base either. Stick to facilities that do what you do, or what you want to do, with similar rates and capabilities.

B. Objectives and Strategy

How will you conquer this market that you just defined? Will you advertise? Will you tailor your services in a certain way? Have you come up with a new way of packaging or pricing that will draw clients? What are your long-term strategic plans?

C. Pricing Policy

Describe all prices and rate structures and indicate how you arrived at them. Explain package deals or block-time rate changes. Indicate outside costs and materials costs that will be charged back to the client.

D. Sales Terms

Describe methods of payment. Cash, checks, credit cards? Deposits up front? Cash-on-delivery? 30-day billing terms for regular clients? What recourse will the business take for terms not complied with?

E. Method of Sales and Distribution

This doesn't look like it would apply to a studio, but it might. Some studios sell products such as telephone message tapes. How are these sold and delivered? What about out-of-state or other remote-location types of business?

F. Customer Service

Will you have a defined customer service policy? Satisfaction guaranteed, no project too small or too large, no deadline too tight?

G. Advertising and Promotion

Indicate all means of projected advertising and promotion used to market the business—periodicals, radio spots, public relations, and so on.

III. Financial Data

A. Proposal

Give a general outline on one page showing how you generated (or will generate) the start-up funds, your projected general income, operating costs, salaries, future expenses, and so on. Use the following sections as a guide, and keep this page brief.

B. Use of Proceeds

1. Sources of Funds

List in numerical order the sources of funds used to start and run the business. Personal investment, business loans, partnership investments, venture capital, lotto winnings, and so on.

2. Use of Proceeds

Indicate in numerical order how funds will be divided. Include construction costs, equipment costs, inventory, salaries, outside services, investments, and so on.

C. Opening Day Balance Sheet

This balance sheet should be on a page of its own in your business plan.

Balance sheet of: [name of business]

As of: [date business opens]

Assets		**Liabilities**	
Cash:	$	Accounts Payable:	$
Inventory:	$	Loans Payable:	$
Owner's equity:			$

D. Start-up Costs

1. Real estate, furniture, fixtures, machinery, equipment

 a. **Purchase Price** [if paid in full with cash] $

 b. **Down Payment** [if paid on contract] $

 c. **Transportation/Installation costs** $

2. Starting Inventory $

3. Decorating and Remodeling $

4. Deposits

a.	Utilities, Telephone	$
b.	Rents	$
c.	Other (specify)	$

5. Fees

a.	Professional (legal, accounting)	$
b.	Licenses, permits, taxes	$
c.	Other (specify)	$

6. Advertising (initial) $

7. Salaries/owner's draw until business opens $

8. Other $

Total Start-up Costs $

E. Monthly Cash-Flow Projection

The table shown in Figure B.1 is a worksheet that can be used to tabulate monthly cash-flow projection. Try to fill out the table for a three-year period. It's OK to be optimistic, but don't portray yourself as a prospective millionaire unless you've got something pretty radical up your sleeve. Use this projection table to gauge your success as the months go by. If you are way above or way below your projected figures, try revising the projections to see where you might be headed. Try to anticipate future purchases of equipment, lulls in activity based on season or other factors, increases in activity, cost increases or increases in your own prices, and so on.

Item	Projected Cost	Dealer A Quote	Dealer B Quote	Actual Paid	Difference
TOTAL					

BUDGET WORKSHEET

Figure B.1   Use this table to calculate monthly cash-flow projections.

After you fill out the projections, make notes and explanations on a separate page, indicating all assumptions made and describing methods used to create the projections.

Finally, you might want to do a break-even analysis. This is nothing more than a chart of your start-up costs versus your net income after expenses each month. This can be used to show when the business actually breaks even and begins to generate profit over your investment.

INDEX

A

absorbers, resonant, 140
access
  maintenance, planning for, 9-10
  planning for, 7-8
acoustic foam, 77
  mounting tiles, 163
acoustics, 131-132
  diffusion, 135
  equalization, 141
  in control rooms, 132-133
  in studios, 142-143
  LEDE (Live End Dead End)
   design, 136-141
  listening and testing, 143-144
  planning for, 10-11
  response measurements, 142
  reverberation time, 133-134
advertising, 196-197
  agencies, 198
  direct-mail marketing, 198-199
  magazines, 198
  press releases, 197
  public relations, 199
  publications, 198

AES (Audio Engineering Society), 23
air conditioning
  construction, 92-93
  planning for, 11-12
alarm systems, 161-162
amplifiers, 51-52
  testing power, 171
analog multitrack tape recorders,
 26-31
  testing, 169-170
audible alarms, 162
audio
  circuits, 104
  for computer-interactive
   media, 188
  for video market
   equipment, 184-186
   synchronization, 186-187
  wire
   budgeting for, 60-62
   routing, 90-91
Aural Exciter, 45-46
automation, mixer considerations, 43
auxiliary sends, mixer
 considerations, 41

B

balanced
   transformers, 108
   wiring, 23, 106-108
bantam connectors, 116
bass traps, 140
bids, 202-203
bit rate, samplers, 37
bookings
   back-to-back, 201-202
   policies, 200
boom stands, budgeting for, 62-63
bridge-mounting monitors, 158-159
brownouts, 103
budget estimates, 64-67
budgeting, 59-60
   audio wire and cable, 60-62
   construction costs, 68-69
   equipment service contracts, 64
   financial plans, 221-225
   furnishings, 63
   insurance, 70-71
   outside services, 63
   patch bays, 124
   related expenses, 69-70
   sales tax, 64
   stands and racks, 62-63
   working with dealers, 71-72
business
   advertising, 196-199
   bids, 202-203
   booking
      policies, 200
      studio time, 201-202
   corporations, 195-196
   limitations, determining, 203-204
   loans, 73
   partnerships, 194-195
   payment policies, 202
   planning for
      access, 7-8
      rest-room facilities, 12
   pricing services, 199-200
   responsibilities and rewards, 2-3
   Small Business Development
      Center, 193
   sole proprietorships, 194
   taxes, 196
   written plans, 193, 211-225
   zoning laws, 3-4, 192

C

C corporations, 195-196
cabinets, equipment, custom,
  156-158
cable, *see* wiring
calibrating tape decks, 180-181
carpeting, 77, 148
cassette-format multitrack tape
  recorders, 26-27
ceilings
   hanging monitors from, 160
   soundproofing, 82-83, 93
chairs, 163-164
channels, mixer considerations,
  40-41
checks, system maintenance, 175-178
cigarette smoking, effects on
  equipment, 182
circuits
   audio, 104
   breakers, 96
   electrical, installing, 103
   grounding, 100-102
   miscellaneous, 112
   separating, 99
cleaning
   dust during finishing work, 147
   tape paths, 178-179
codes
   LTC (Longitudinal Time Code),
     186, 187
   SMPTE time, 186-187
   VITC (Vertical Interval Time
     Code), 38, 186, 187
collective absorption coefficient, 134

commercial studios, *see* business
compatibility of equipment, 22-23
compressors, 45
    testing, 170
computer-interactive media, audio
    for, 188
computers as sequencing machines,
    33-34
concrete, 78
condenser microphones, 53
connectors, bantam, 116
consoles, *see* mixing consoles
construction
    budget estimates, 67
    calculating costs, 68-69
    climate control, 92-93
    equipment racks, 91, 150-151
        metal cage, 151-153
        wallmount, 153-154
    headphone distribution system,
        111-112
    isolation booths, 89-90
    materials, 76-79
    soundproofing
        ceilings, 82-83, 93
        doors, 88-89
        walls, 80-82, 93
        windows, 84-88, 93
    walls, 79-80
    wire routing, 90-91
control
    panels, 162
    rooms
        acoustic response
            measurements, 142
        acoustics, 132-133
        diffusion, 135-141
        equalization, 141
        layout examples, 12-18
        reverberation time, 133-134
        space for, 5-7
        wiring requirements, 105
controllers, 34
conventions, 23-24

corporations, 195-196
costs
    mixers, 43-44
    patch bays, 124-125
    written plans, 221-225
crosstalk, mixer considerations,
    42-43
current, 97

D

DATs (digital audio tapes), 46
DAWs (Digital Audio
    Workstations), 47-49
DBA (Doing Business As), 194
dealers, working with, 71-72
demagnetizers, 55
demagnetizing tape heads, 179-180
diffusion, 135
digitizing images, 189
dimmers, 102
direct-mail marketing, 198-199
DMMs (digital multimeters), 55
doors, soundproofing, 88-89
DSPs (Digital Signal Processors), 44
dust, cleaning during finishing
    work, 147
dynamic microphones, 53
dynamics processors, 45

E

early reflections, 132-133
effects, 44-45
    sends, mixer considerations, 41
electrical
    budgeting for, 70
    circuits, installing, 103
    services, budgeting for, 63
    wiring, *see* power
EMI filters, 177
entrance service panels, 96
EQ section, mixer considerations, 42
equalization, 141
equalizers, 45

equipment
    analog multitrack tape recorders, 26-31
    budget estimates, 65-66
    cabinets, 156-158
    compatibility, 22-23
    Digital Audio Workstations, 47-49
    effects of smoking, 182
    furniture, 163-164
    installing, 173-175
    layout and ergonomics, planning for, 11
    maintenance, 55-56, 178-181
        access, planning for, 9-10
        budgeting for, 69-70
        checks, 175-178
    microphones, 53-54
    MIDI sequencing, 31-35
    mixdown decks, 46
    mixing consoles, 39-44
    mounting monitors, 158-160
    near-field monitoring, 49-52
    outboard effects, 44-45
    paperwork, 171-172
    power requirements, 97-98
    racks and stands
        construction, 91, 150-154
        empty spaces, 154-156
        grounding considerations, 148-150
        standard space for, 148
    recording process components, 24-26
    repairing, 181-182
        budgeting for, 69-70
    samplers, 35-37
    service contracts, budgeting for, 64
    state-of-the-art, 23-24
    synchronizers, 38
    TDS (Time-Delay Spectrometry), 142
    testing, 55-56, 167-171
    unpacking, 166-167
    VCRs, 185
    video, 188-190
ergonomics, planning for, 11
expanders, 45

F

fader automation, moving, 43
fans, muffin, 152-153
fiberglass insulation, 79
files on equipment maintenance, 172
financial plans, 221-225
    see also budgeting
financing
    business loans, 73
    home equity loans, 73
    unsecured personal loans, 72
    venture capital, 73-74
fixed-frequency oscillators, 55
flat responses, 50
floor stands, mounting monitors, 158
flooring, 148
floppy disks, storing sampler sounds, 37
fluorescent lighting, 102
flush-mounted monitors, acoustics, 137
foam panels, 77
Fostex multitrack tape recorders, 27-30
free-standing monitors, acoustics, 137
furnishings, 163-164
    budgeting for, 63
fuses, testing, 168-169

G

gates, noise, 45
gen-locking, 188
generators, sound, 34-35
graphics, video, 188-190
ground loops, 100
    when patching, 120

grounding
  circuits, 100-102
  eliminating problems at
    equipment installation, 173-174
  racks and stands, 148-150
  transient noise caused by
    peripheral equipment, 177-178
gypsum board, 78

H

half-normal configuration patch
  bays, 118
hard disk recorders, 48
hard drives, storing sampler
  sounds, 37
HDTV (High Definition
  Television), 188
headphones, wiring distribution
  system, 111-112
headroom, 22
heads
  aligning, 180-181
  cleaning, 178-179
  demagnetizing, 179-180
heating
  budgeting for, 70
  construction, 92-93
  overheating in equipment
    racks, 152
  planning for, 11-12
high-frequency noise, eliminating
  problems at equipment
  installation, 174-175
home equity loans, 73

I

in-line consoles, 39
inaudible alarms, 162
input
  channels, mixer considerations,
    40-41
  fuses, testing, 168-169
  stations, wiring, 109-110

installing equipment, 173-175
instruction manuals, 172
insulation, fiberglass, 79
insurance, budgeting for, 70-71
interior traps, 162
isolation booths
  construction, 89-90
  planning for, 12

J-K

jacks, 119-120
  phone and telephone, 129

keyboard, testing, 170

L

labels, wiring, 109
laws, zoning, 192
layouts
  equipment, planning for, 11
  examples, 12-18
  patch bays, 120-123
LEDE (Live End Dead End) control
  room design, 136-141
lighting, 102
Line signal level, 22
loans
  business, 73
  home equity, 73
  unsecured personal, 72
  venture capital, 73-74
lost equipment, 166-167
LTC (Longitudinal Time Code),
  186-187
lumber in construction, 78

M

Macintosh computers as sequencing
  machines, 33-34
magazines, 198
  list of, 207-208
magnetometers, 180

maintenance
    access, planning for, 9-10
    budgeting for, 69-70
    calibrating tape decks, 180-181
    checks, 175
        console, 175-176
        multitrack, 175-176
        patch bays, 176-178
        peripheral equipment, 176-178
        studio, 176
    cleaning tape paths, 178-179
    demagnetizing tape heads,
      179-180
    equipment, 55-56
    files on equipment, 172
manuals, instruction, 172
marketing plans, 218-220
metal cage equipment rack
  construction, 151-153
microphones, 53-54
    mounting, 160
MIDI (Musical Instrument Digital
  Interface)
    for computer-interactive
      media, 188
    sequencing equipment, 31-35
Mike signal level, 22
minimum advance notices, 200
missing equipment, 166-167
mixdown decks, 46
mixing consoles (mixers), 39-44
    maintenance checks, 175-176
    testing, 171
modal frequencies, 131
monitoring
    area, *see* control rooms
    near-field, 49-52
monitors
    flush-mounted versus
      free-standing, 137
    mounting, 158-160
moving fader automation, 43
muffin fans, 152-153

multimedia
    audio
        for computer-interactive
          media, 188
        for video market, 184-187
    future of, 190
    history of, 183-184
    video standards and graphics,
      188-190
multitrack
    maintenance checks, 175-176
    tape recorders, 26-31
mults, 118

N

NAMM (National Association
  of Musical Equipment
  Manufacturers), 23
near-field monitoring, 49-52
    mounting monitors, 158-160
noise
    caused by
        electrical appliances, 99
        electromagnetic energy,
          106-107
        fluorescent lighting, 102
        heating/cooling ductwork,
          92-93
        patch bays, 123
        peripheral equipment, 177-178
    eliminating at equipment
      installation
        ground hum, 173-174
        high-frequency, 174-175
    floor, mixer considerations, 42-43
    gates, 45
    reducing
        by short cable runs, 104
        with balanced wiring, 108
        with carpeting, 77
        with grounding wires, 100-101
        with multitrack tape machines,
          28-29

normal configuration patch bays, 117-118
NTSC video standard, 188

O

open configuration patch bays, 116-117
open-reel multitrack tape recorders, 26
oscillators, 55
oscilloscopes, 55
outboard effects, 44-45

P

packing materials, saving, 172
paperwork on equipment, 171-172
parallel configuration patch bays, 118
partnership agreements, 195
partnerships, 194-195
patch bays, 115-116
    cost, 124-125
    laying out, 120-123
    maintenance checks, 176-178
    patch cords, 129
    plugs and jacks, 129
    soldering, 125-128
    types, 116-120
payment policies, 202
peripheral equipment, maintenance checks, 176-178
personal loans, unsecured, 72
phantom power, 41
phase grating diffusers, 135
phone jacks, 129
plenums, 92
plug-in-type lamps, 102
plugs, phone and telephone, 129
plumbing, planning for, 12
portastudios, 26
postproduction, 185-186
potentiometers, 111

power, 97
    amplifiers, testing, 171
    circuits
        audio, 104
        electrical, installing, 103
        grounding, 100-102
        miscellaneous, 112
        separating, 99
    constructing headphone distribution system, 111-112
    lighting, 102
    requirements, 97-98
    studio input stations, 109-110
    voltage fluctuations, 103
    wiring
        balanced versus unbalanced, 106-108
        labelling, 109
        requirements, 104-106
        room diagram, 96
        routing, 90-91
        types, 108-109
power-line conditioners, 103
press releases, 197
pricing services, 199-200
processors, 44-45
    signal, testing, 170
project studios
    design types, 4-5
    layout examples, 12-18
    running as businesses,
        see business
    space
        planning, 7-12
        use of, 5-7
proposed budgets, 64-67
psychoacoustic processors, 45
public relations, 199
publications, 198
    list of, 207-208

Q-R

quality, 203-204

rack rails, 150-151
racks
    budgeting for, 62-63
    constructing, 150-151
        metal cage, 151-153
        wallmount, 153-154
    construction, 91
    empty spaces, 154-156
    grounding considerations,
      148-150
    standard space for, 148
recessed ceiling fixtures, 102
recording
    area, *see* studios
    consoles, *see* mixing consoles
    process, 24-26
reflections, early, 132-133
repairing
    budgeting for, 69-70
    equipment, 181-182
resilient channels, 82
resonances, 141
resonant absorbers, 140
rest-room facilities, planning for, 12
reverberation time, 133-134
RFZ (Reflection-Free Zone), 138-141
RGB (RedGreenBlue) format, 189
ribbon microphones, 53
ring connection, 119
rock wool, 159
room volume, 134
rough estimate budgets, 64-67

S

sales tax, budgeting for, 64
samplers, 35-37
sampling
    rate, 37
    time, 37
saving packing materials, 172
security systems, 161
    audible and inaudible alarms, 162

control panels, 162
sensors, 161-162
sequencing software, 31-33
service contracts, equipment
    budgeting for, 64
    working with dealers, 72
service panels
    entrance, 96
    separating circuits, 99
services
    budgeting for outside work, 63
    pricing, 199-200
Sheetrock, 78
shipping materials, saving, 172
shock-mount microphone
  holders, 160
signal
    levels, 22
    processors, testing, 170
Small Business Development
  Center, 193
smoking, effects on equipment, 182
Society of Motion Picture and
  Television Engineers (SMPTE), 24
    time code, 186-187
soffitmount monitors, 159
soffits, 159
software, sequencing, 31-33
solder wick, 126
solder-suckers, 126
soldering
    irons, 125
    techniques, 126-128
    tools, 125-126
    vises, 126
solderpullit, 126
sole proprietorships, 194
Sonic Maximizers, 45
sound, 76
    cues, 185-186
    generators, 34-35
        testing, 170
    locks, 88-89
    mixer quality, 40

soundproofing
  ceilings, 82-83, 93
  doors, 88-89
  planning for, 8
  walls, 80-82, 93
  windows, 84-88, 93
space
  empty, in equipment racks, 154-156
  layout examples, 12-18
  mixer considerations, 41-42
  planning for
    access, 7-8
    acoustics, 10-11
    equipment layout and ergonomics, 11
    heating, ventilation, and air conditioning, 11-12
    isolation booths, 12
    maintenance access, 9-10
    rest-room facilities, 12
    soundproofing, 8
    wire routing, 9
  use of, 5-7
speakers, 50
split consoles, 39
standards, NTSC video, 188
stands
  budgeting for, 62-63
  grounding considerations, 148-150
  mounting monitors, 158-160
  standard space for, 148
start-up, written plans for, 221-225
state-of-the-art equipment, 23-24
STC (Sound Transmission Coefficient), 79-80
studio time
  booking, 201-202
  payment policies, 202
  pricing, 199-200
studios
  acoustics, 142-143
  input stations, wiring, 109-110

layout examples, 12-18
maintenance checks, 176
space for, 5-7
wiring requirements, 105
Subchapter S corporations, 195
subgroups, mixer considerations, 41
supplies, budgeting for, 70
surges
  clamping, 103
  suppressors, 98
sweet spot, 138-141
sweetening, 184
synchronization, 186-187
synchronizers, 38
system maintenance checks, 175-178

T

talent rooms, *see* studios
tape
  decks
    calibrating, 180-181
    testing, 169-170
  paths
    cleaning, 178-179
    demagnetizing, 179-180
  recorders, multitrack, 26-31
  sends, 117
tape-based digital recorders, 48
Tascam multitrack tape recorders, 27-31
tax numbers, 196
taxes, 196
  sales, budgeting for, 64
TBCs (TimeBase Correctors), 189
TDS (Time-Delay Spectrometry) equipment, 142
technical assistance, budgeting for, 63
telephone
  jacks, 129
  plugs, 129
  services, budgeting for, 63

testing equipment, 167-169
   analog tape decks, 169-170
   console, 171
   equipment for, 55-56
   power amplifiers, 171
   signal processors, 170
   sound generators, 170
three-contact jacks, 119
time-arrival misinformation, 141
track lighting, 102
trade shows, 23-24
two-contact jacks, 119

U-V

unbalanced wiring, 23, 106-108
unpacking equipment, 166-167
unsecured personal loans, 72

VCA (voltage controlled amplifier)
  automation, 43
VCRs, 185
ventilation, planning for, 11-12
venture capital, 73-74
video
   audio for, 184-187
     games, 188
   standards and graphics, 188-190
Video Toaster, 190
VITC (Vertical Interval Time Code),
  38, 186-187
voltage fluctuations, 103

W

wallboard, 78
wallmount
   equipment rack construction,
    153-154
   monitors, 159-160
walls
   acoustic foam tiles, 163
   construction techniques, 79-80
   finishing work, 147
   soundproofing, 80-82, 93

warranties, 171-172
weather stripping, 77
windows, soundproofing, 84-88, 93
wiring
   balanced, 23
     versus unbalanced, 106-108
   budgeting for, 60-62
   labelling, 109
   requirements, 104-106
   routing, 90-91
     planning for, 9
   types, 108-109
   unbalanced, 23
wood in construction, 78
workspace, *see* space
workstations
   DAWs (Digital Audio
    Workstations), 47-49
   MIDI, 32-33

X-Z

Z channels, 83-84
zip cords, 109
zoning
   laws, 3-4, 192
   variances, 192